Learning to Forgive

Doris Donnelly

Abingdon Press   Nashville

LEARNING TO FORGIVE

Copyright © 1979 by Doris Donnelly

This book is printed on recycled acid-free paper.

ISBN 0-687-21324-X

(previously published by Macmillan under ISBN 0-02-532140-4 and by Abingdon Press under ISBN 0-687-21323-1)

PRINTED IN THE UNITED STATES OF AMERICA

93 94 95 96 97 98 99 00 01 02 03 — 15 14 13 12 11 10

LEARNING TO FORGIVE

To my Mother

CONTENTS

ACKNOWLEDGMENTS

So many people helped me with this book that I feel it is not entirely my own. I cannot mention the names of all, but I would first like to thank Bill Griffin, mostly my friend but also my editor at Macmillan, who pursued me and this project as if he were the spirit who hovered over the dark, empty, and endless void. I also thank Rita Carney and Rosemarie McGinty for their assistance and suggestions. And Jim Joy and Doug Holladay for the encouragement and friendship they provided along the way.

I am especially grateful for the clarity and guidance provided by Jim Loder, my colleague at Princeton Theological Seminary, who helped me steer the course I chose. And I am also grateful to Msgr. Howard W. McCormick and the New England Congress of Religious Educators, who invited me to return to speak at Hartford and Springfield and Amherst and Holyoke, and at the same time gave me the opportunity to rethink and refine some of the thoughts contained herein.

In the end, I am grateful to Irene Hatrak and Rosemarie Micharski, women of extraordinary generosity, who gave me lots more than a superbly typed manuscript.

ACKNOWLEDGMENTS

And lastly, there are my children, Christopher and Peggy, two very gentle peacemakers, who created the atmosphere of joy and love in which this book was born.

Princeton, New Jersey
March 17, 1979

INTRODUCTION

Not until 1966 was there a separate entry in *The Reader's Guide to Periodical Literature* under the word "Failure." Up to that time, anyone searching for "Failure" would find "Failure—see Success."

A preoccupation with success—striving for it, attaining it, preserving it—obscures the reality of failure in human life and obscures the need for forgiveness, too, because forgiveness presupposes failure and attempts to be creative about it.

Forgiveness is an invitation to redeem failure. Without forgiveness, we would never be released from the consequences of what we have done or what has been done to us, and "our capacity to act would, as it were, be confined to one single deed from which we could never recover."[1]

Yet for whatever allure and redemptive value forgiveness possesses, it is also so disturbingly unreasonable as to make us question its feasibility and the world's readiness for it. A forgiveness that claims our sins, though scarlet, to be made as white as snow, is a proclamation of so radical a kind as to border on the fantastic.

H.R. Mackintosh once asked whether forgiveness was

immoral, unnecessary, and/or impossible.[2] At one time or another, most of us have asked similar questions about forgiveness, and this book hopes never to lose sensitivity to those questions.

As well as establishing an awareness of the difficulties connected with forgiveness, these pages deal mostly with the formidable power that forgiveness exercises in our lives which enables us to acknowledge that the decisions of human life, even when they turn out badly, are not above repair. It is a book about the uncommon, uncompromising, and unpredictable promise that forgiveness offers to us all.

LEARNING
TO FORGIVE

CHAPTER I

Bypassing Forgiveness

Some years ago, I watched as a thirteen-year-old boy was returned to the custody of his parents. It was a disturbing transaction.

After the father mumbled a few words to the presiding judge, the parents and son passed through the courthouse corridors, down the many staircases, and across several streets to their car for the ride home. During the course of this long walk, not a word was spoken. Nor was there an embrace or even a handshake. These hurt and hurting people even avoided eye contact with each other.

When they got to their house, the father announced, "Things will be different from now on." Then he turned and left to spend his day elsewhere. The mother tidily hung her coat in the hall closet and went to the kitchen where she kept busy for the rest of the afternoon. The son stretched out on a sofa. Two younger sisters came by and gawked. He pulled a throw cushion over his face and groaned.

Technically, a reconciliation had occurred. The son and his parents were reunited, brought together. But this was about as far from a lasting reconciliation as one could possibly imagine.

I was sent to the court that morning by the private school the son had been attending when he ran away from home three months before. The school promised readmission, and I was there to confirm that message.

He ran away again two weeks later. "We did everything we could for him," the mother told me. "We even bought him a new stereo the day he left. What went wrong?"

Many things, I suppose. One of those things is the subject of this book.

I've relived this experience many times. Over the years I've come to see that it is typical of one way many of us have of solving a certain kind of problem. That way is to move swiftly from our hurt to a reconciliation without taking stock of the wounds that have been inflicted—that is, without noticing our emotional responses—and without appreciating the pivotal place that forgiveness holds in the process.

Forgiveness is part of a process that begins with a hurt and ends, as its final and long-range goal, with the event of reconciliation. To reconcile means to bring together that which belongs together but which is apart; it works only when we pause to forgive, only when we become aware of the depths of the offense against us so that we can forgive with all our wits about us and ensure an enduring peace.

Most of the time, we bypass forgiveness. Most of the time, like the parents in this story, we race with lightning speed from our hurts to reconciliation without taking a look at what must be forgiven before lasting healing can take hold.

The fact of the matter is that we've been programmed since childhood not to nurse our wounds, to keep a stiff upper lip, to pretend that we are unaffected by other people's cruelty, deliberate or accidental—in other words, we are programmed to bypass forgiveness.

That etiquette is reinforced ritually by a series of gestures that allow us to do bypass surgery on our hurts and emotions. We can probably all remember a parent somewhere directing little children to "kiss and make up" or a mediator either coaching two friends to "shake hands," or encouraging estranged adults to "hurry and get together again." The premium has been on speed. The quicker we move away from our grief, the better. Better still, not to notice it at all, we are told.

To do the opposite—to confront our hurts, to face our wounds head-on—has often been regarded as an embarrassing act of self-serving pity. There's very little room within this expected, conforming behavior for someone saying, "I know what you did. Your jealousy, your lies, cost me my job, gave me an ulcer, turned my wife's hair gray, and made me so ashamed of my failure that I drank myself into oblivion every night." Bypassing forgiveness spares us all that. It allows us to suppress and repress our hurts and to bury our resentments.

The pattern of behavior that inspires people inspires nations, too. After barbaric and inhuman behavior among countries, we have seen those same nations sit down at the conference table to sign treaties in a noble tribute to

3

reconciliation. We have seen those very same truces violated before the ink is dry when countries have not forgiven before reconciliation is attempted. If brother does not forgive brother, and friend does not forgive friend, and nation does not forgive nation, then all the handshakes and kisses and signed treaties are worthless.

The leader of a foreign government recently undertook a peace mission to an enemy country. It was heralded as a heroic and magnanimous overture of good will, of detente, of possible reconciliation—but its strength and impact was short-lived. Soon after the visit, one country began warring on the other almost as if the reconciling gesture hadn't happened. What hadn't happened, of course, was forgiveness. To hasten reconciliation without allowing the two sides to unveil and examine their wounds, and then, in the light of day, to forgive the making of those wounds—that is, to "reconcile" without wrestling with and coming to terms with forgiveness—is a futile, patch-up gesture doomed to allow the original hurt to fester again in short order with even greater violence. Peace, in families, in friendships, and among nations, is a costly business, and the price is exercising the uncommon behavior known as forgiveness.

Several years ago, Gerald Ford opened the floodgates of criticism and popular censure when, as president, he pardoned Richard Nixon. President Ford later defended his action by claiming it an act of kindness and charity—and well it might have been. Yet the nation was not ready for that gesture, and three years later there were those willing to suggest that that act of kindness cost Gerald Ford an election.

In theological terms, we could say that what President Ford did was offer to reconcile ex-President Nixon with the nation before its citizens were able to forgive. Reconciliation seemed inappropriate, like an arm around the shoulder of a wounded country before the shrapnel could be picked out and the wound cleaned and bandaged—that is, while the nation awaited healing. It seemed premature and peremptory, and the nation sensed the discrepancy.

Whatever technical and legal distinctions were made between guilt and pardon, there seems to be little doubt that the mood of the country was not ready to be reconciled until the people could at least touch base with forgiveness. This does not have to be viewed as a vindictive, vengeful, retaliatory need; it is likely to have been none of these things, and more a need for a fitting pause before trust and love could take root again.

We all know (to move away from national and international episodes) of home and family situations where husbands and wives, fathers and sons, sisters and brothers, mothers-in-law and daughters-in-law, and all mixtures in-between, live on a superficial level of reconciliation without ever having forgiven. There are the seasonal phone calls, the antiseptic birthday remembrances; but the resentments have been buried so deeply that there is no joy in these meetings. No heart.

There are situations, of course, where neither reconciliation nor forgiveness takes place—where persons absent themselves from each other's presence for a lifetime. Sometimes a hostess attempts a reconciliatory gathering of the clan only to be rebuffed with "If *they* are coming, count me out." The need for forgiveness is pervasive and constant. Where it is present, there is a quality to life that is tension-less and grace-full. Where it is missing, there are gnarled and hardened lives frequently slushing around in self-pitying, self-righteous behavior.

One of the insidious consequences of bypassing forgiveness is allowing the impression that since we seem to be able to glide with ease from the hurt to reconciliation, forgiveness must be easy. In the closing pages of *The Hiding Place,* evangelist Corrie ten Boom tells a story that helps us understand that it just isn't so.

After her release from a concentration camp where her sister Betsie died, Corrie ten Boom lectured and preached on the need to forgive our enemies. The struggle with the command to forgive was brought home with stunning force when, after one of her guest preachings, Corrie was greeted by a man whom she recognized as the SS guard at the shower room in the processing center at Ravensbruck.

How grateful I am for your message, Fräulein," he said. "To think that, as you say, He has washed my sins away!"

And suddenly, it was all there—the roomful of mocking men, the heaps of clothing, Betsie's pain-blanched face.

His hand was thrust out to shake mine. And I, who had preached so often to the people in Bloemendaal the need to forgive, kept my hand at my side.

Even as the angry, vengeful thoughts boiled through me, I saw the sin of them. Jesus Christ had died for this man; was I going to ask for more? Lord Jesus, I prayed, forgive me and help me to forgive him.

I tried to smile. I struggled to raise my hand. I could not. I felt nothing, not the slightest spark of warmth or charity. And so again I breathed a silent prayer. Jesus I cannot forgive him. Give me Your forgiveness.

As I took his hand a most incredible thing happened. From my shoulder along my arm and through my hand a current seemed to pass from me to him, while into my heart sprang a love for this stranger that almost overwhelmed me.

And so I discovered that it is not on our forgiveness any more than on our goodness that the world's healing hinges, but on His. When He tells us to love our enemies, He gives, along with the command, the love itself.[1]

Corrie ten Boom's story tells us that the practice of forgiveness is harder than its theory. It tells us that there's nothing instinctive or, God knows, easy about it. This woman took the business of forgiveness seriously. She did not pretend reconciliation. She considered the depths of her hurts, her traumas, her fears, and her wounds. She took inventory. She felt. She hurt. And she said in her speechlessness and temporary paralysis that she needed empowerment from a source not her own to do what had to be done.

Hundreds of years ago, Jesus told another story about a non-forgiver with a similar ring of authenticity about it. It is told within a story of two brothers and a father so prodigal that he upstages the non-forgiving dimension to the story.[2] The younger of the two brothers early on asks for his share of an inheritance and leaves with it to experience life in a mood reminiscent of a sailor on leave in Tijuana.

There is reason to suspect that he is needed at home, agrarian societies being, as they were, dependent on the cooperative efforts and strengths of young men. There is reason to believe that the son who stays at home is burdened by his brother's absence. And there is also reason to suspect that the son's absence leaves the father grief-stricken, with his heart empty, longing for the day his son might return. The story explicitly tells us that the father is the one who first spots his son walking on the trail up to the house, probably because he always looked through the windows whenever he passed them, in the hope that someday he would see his son return.

That kind of vigilant, expansive love empowers the father to welcome the return of his son unconditionally. Amazingly the father does not hesitate, does not pause. In an extraordinary burst of forgiving love, he knows what his son has done, he offers a homecoming, chooses to cover his son's embarrassment, and receives him with no holds barred.

The father could, of course, have extracted a promise about future behavior. He could have mandated an appropriate punishment—some kind of exclusion from the inner sanctum of the family, a thought which, it would appear, occurs to the younger son on his way home: "He can treat me as one of the hired servants." But the father does no such thing.

Unlike Corrie ten Boom, the father's arms are not frozen and they reach immediately to embrace the hurts, the tears, and the time that this renegade son "was lost and is now found." But after all, the father in this parable is there to tell us how God (and not ordinary people) acts with sinners, and the story is meant to illustrate prodigality. It is a model of outlandish behavior indeed, and behavior that was meant to be understood as lavish and unusual. Untypical, certainly, by human standards.

Far more typical is the behavior of the elder brother. Hurt by his brother's absence, burdened by laboring in his stead, and deeply offended by the big welcome planned and executed by the father, the older brother finds it hard going to forgive.

As in the story of Corrie ten Boom, perhaps what the elder son and brother is saying here is "Not yet," "Not now," "Maybe later." And, as in the story of the parents who regained custody of their son, maybe what the elder son needs is the vision that the reconciliation will be built on sand unless forgiveness takes place. Perhaps, after all, what the elder brother is saying is "Give me time—I'm only human."

What we know for sure is that we have here an incomplete parable. The ending may well be that the older brother forgives his brother and his father *eventually*. It could be that his hesitation might be read as a healthy sign, an indication that the elder brother is not about to bury his wounds with a pretense at reconciliation. Nor is he about to brush off the homecoming episode with an insincere but socially acceptable "Don't mention it—I didn't even notice you were gone."

Yet, in time, the older brother may have done what Corrie ten Boom was able to do and what the parents and their thirteen-year-old son needed to do: lean on someone else's love. He would wind up, then, being propelled and impelled by a power greater than his anger, or jealousy, or envy, or pain, or suffering. In the process, those hurts that loomed so large would become smaller, more manageable, and would tyrannize him less.

But that's the end of our story, and we're still at the beginning. We have recognized the need for forgiveness and the tragedy of bypassing it. There is another tragedy associated with forgiveness, and that involves denying it deliberately and consciously to those who have hurt us. People who don't forgive offer convincing reasons for this style of living. We will take a look at some of those reasons in the next chapter.

9

CHAPTER II

Why People
Don't Forgive

OR MANY PEOPLE, the question about forgiveness isn't how or when, but whether it's even possible. The truth of the matter is that for many people, the pain of a hurt is so deep, and the connecting anger, hatred, or resentment so profound, that forgiveness doesn't seem to be a likely possibility. At least, not for a long time. For many people, non-forgiveness seems to be the only reasonable way.

It is probably true that non-forgiveness *is* the only reasonable way. It honors the emotions, it affirms rather than denies pain and its aftereffects, and it looks after the person who was damaged in the scuffle.

Forgiveness, on the other hand, is *un*reasonable. Life, of course, is also frequently unreasonable, and so, too, is God. Children die, husbands leave their wives (and wives their husbands), old people die lonely, floods wipe out communities, fortunes are passed on to ruthless men and women, and God appears to allow these tragedies without interfering with or countermanding the powers of a world that is ultimately within His control. Yet it is only the person who experiences and survives the unreasonableness of life who can understand the unreasonableness of forgiveness. Once that is understood, mystery is born— and forgiveness is, at its heart, a mystery.

There is, on the other hand, no mystery about non-forgiveness. It stands clearly as the logical, appropriate, instinctive, normal, natural, and proper response to offenses and hurts that bore deep scars in our lives. We owe it to ourselves and to posterity to teach those who have wronged us the error of their ways and the fact that we won't allow reconciliation to be a simple matter. To top it all off, the non-forgiver has a lot of support from the surrounding community; there's many a person around who would bolster our decision not to let the scoundrel off without exacting our due.

When all is said and done, there are basically six reasons why people don't forgive. We should be able to recognize in this compact number of reasons why we ourselves are tempted not to forgive, and why we are able to empathize so fully with those of our friends who find forgiveness tough going.

People Don't Forgive Because the Pain Is New and Deep

When the pain is fresh and raw and deep, it's very hard to forgive. A loving and supportive husband whose wife abandons him and their three sons will not be able to forget the grief she has caused and remember her with affection. At least not immediately.

Even when the pain is older and more seasoned, forgiveness is not an easy business. A friend of a friend of mine whose mother's illness was misdiagnosed by a physician and whose mother subsequently suffered brain damage because of an improper surgical-anesthesiological procedure, was not only unconsoled when she was awarded over two million dollars in a malpractice suit, but the court award exacerbated her pain because it forced her to remember and reopen wounds in her own life that were trying to be healed. This friend's friend told me that the horrible resentment she felt toward her mother's physician was triggered every time she passed a car with an "MD" license plate. Throughout the hearing on the case, this woman could not bear the thought of extending forgiveness to the person responsible, even though her mother was making some progress.

A neighbor of mine, a husband and father of four, was unable to forgive his business partner of twenty-five years for misusing money from their small company to pay off huge personal debts. Their company, having coped with innumerable reverses because of this unrevealed financial skullduggery, will not be able to survive the latest loss of capital and is currently filing for bankruptcy.

In addition to dealing with his own feelings of betrayal, my neighbor and his partner are facing legal suits from their creditors that both of them are technically liable for. Furthermore, my friend has to contend with college-tuition bills, an unpaid mortgage, unpromising career alternatives, substantial legal fees, and the personal emotional stress this situation has placed on his wife, for whom the social stigma of these events has led to a paralyzing depression.

For the time being, my neighbor is not able to forgive. His blood boils when he thinks of his partner and the lies he was told over the last five years to cover the fraud. He is embittered when associates call to confirm their dislike of his partner and remind him of the opportunities they once offered to him to go into business with them. And his hands tremble when he opens the mail each morning and sorts through the bills that he is unable to pay. He is consumed by a feeling of failure, unable to empathize at all with his business partner's realistic fear of a prison term. He feels guilty and resentful and filled with inconsolable pain. These are all healings that will require time and plenty of support.

Affirming the hurt at the beginning, and claiming the pain, acknowledges the parameters of what has to be dealt with, and it takes the business of forgiving seriously. The person who attends to pain in this fashion—realistically, and without excess drama—will allow others to emote, to sound out their hurts and pains and grievances, and will be sensitive to the right moment to encourage a forgiving and healing process.

It is no easy thing to love our neighbors—a command at the heart of Christianity. It is surely no easy thing to love our neighbors when we are hurting. That is the goal, to be sure; but it is a goal that requires practice and exercise to claim, and strategies to reach, and support from a community to sustain. It is this goal, however, that permanent non-forgivers forever deny, and in so doing deny themselves a life free from pain.

What we are saying about pain—fresh, new, old, deep, wounding—is that it is part of the human condition. The forgiver and non-forgiver both experience it. The forgiver will eventually choose to move beyond it; the non-forgiver will make his or her home there everlastingly. And it is the unrelenting pull of that pain that in itself does not allow us to emerge from its depths to console the afflictor with words of forgiveness.

People Don't Forgive Because of Anger, Jealousy, Resentment

The second reason people don't forgive is because of a range of emotions which they feel toward their enemies. The most popular and powerful of these are anger, jealousy, and resentment.

When anger is strong and overt, and of the destructive variety, it is frequently allied with revenge and retaliation. A young woman was about to park her car when the driver of another car, a young man, swooped into the parking place that she was waiting for. Recognizing that he had stolen her place, he smiled and blew her a kiss. Infuriated, she found herself another parking place, returned to the young man's car, and let the air out of his tires! Anger. Revenge. Retaliation. No room for forgiveness here!

Sometimes the anger remains strong, but its focus—the real issue—is concealed from the offending party. For example, a mother was angry when her twenty-one-year-old daughter moved to her own apartment. The mother camouflaged her anger under a veil of concern for her daughter's safety and statistics about the crime rate in her daughter's new neighborhood, but the real issue—the "hidden agenda"—was that the mother was angry that (1) she would be left alone; (2) her daughter would be having fun while she was depressed; and (3) her daughter was growing up and she no longer had control over her life.

The place that forgiveness plays in this process rests with the mother's coming to terms with forgiving her daughter's independence and adulthood. The daughter, too, is in the position of forgiving her mother for the unreasonable expectations the mother placed on her.

In a very perceptive article, James Lapsley takes up this theme when he talks of forgiveness and "lost contracts."[1] Contracts, in this case, are those arrangements which we *assume* we have with other people. We expect those people to live up to them—whether they know it or not. Lapsley argues that these contracts have to be surrendered, and people forgiven for being human, before relationships can resume on a healthy and solid footing.

Hidden agendas are very hard to work through for the precise reason that they *are* hidden. An ardent women's libber confessed to a woman who directed a large government agency, "It took me years to forgive you for being a woman in such a visible and influential position who didn't directly take up the cause I saw as so important." Here, too, the need is to forgive the expectations we have of one another, to cancel contracts that bind instead of allow people to be themselves.

Jealousy—the jealousy that does not allow me to rejoice with the joy of another—is still another emotion that disables forgiveness.

A particularly illustrative example is the Old Testament story of Jonah. When Jonah was commissioned by Yahweh to preach repentance to the Ninevites, a people he disdained with passion, he went instead in the opposite direction to Tarshish. Jonah's dislike of the people of Nineveh was so intense, his hatred so real, that the worse thing he could imagine was that they would listen to him, repent, and be friends of Yahweh. He could not bear to think that if that were to happen he might be considered responsible in some small measure for mediating their salvation. Jonah felt the inhabitants of Nineveh unworthy prospects for Yahweh's mercy, forgiveness, and blessing— a thought fortunately not shared by Yahweh himself.

Jonah was a man consumed by resentment, a man who did not see eye-to-eye with Yahweh's magnanimity in sparing the city and its inhabitants if they would repent and turn from their evil ways. He was a man who desired not the salvation but destruction of the Ninevites, and he tried with vigor to thwart Yahweh's master plan—to no end.

After Jonah's detour in the belly of a great fish, he finally obeyed Yahweh's command, preached to the Ninevites, and saw the result of his preaching: every person repented. Jonah felt bitter and weary because the Ninevites were saved from what Jonah felt they deserved.

In the final episode, Jonah went to lie down outside the city and was comforted, temporarily, by the shade of an ivy plant. To Jonah's utter disappointment the tree withered overnight, yet Jonah did not recognize the irony of his concern over the destruction of a mere plant in light of his indifference to the destruction of an entire city (had the message of Yahweh not been preached to them).

In a similar vein, Louis Evely recounts the story of Jean Anouilh's play, *The Last Judgment*, where

> The good are densely clustered at the gate of heaven,
>   eager to march in,
>   sure of their reserved seats,
>   keyed up and bursting with impatience.
> All at once, a rumor starts spreading:
>   "It seems he's going to forgive those others, too!"
> For a minute, everyone's dumbfounded.
> They look at one another in disbelief,
>   gasping and sputtering,

"After all the trouble I went through!"
"If only I'd known this . . . !"
"I just can't get over it!"
Exasperated, they work themselves into a frenzy
    and start cursing God;
    and at that very instant they're damned!
Love appeared,
    and they refused to acknowledge it.
"We don't know this man!"
"We don't approve of a heaven
that's open to every Tom, Dick, and Harry!"
"We spurn a God who lets everyone off!"
"We can't love a God who loves so foolishly."
And because they didn't love Love,
    they didn't recognize him.[2]

Jonah's tale and Anouilh's play recount an exceedingly human predicament: Why should I, at the moment of singular advantage, declare the score even and allow you to share the benefits that I want to belong only to me?

The word *resentment* is derived from the Latin *re-sentire* ("to feel again"). The non-forgiver, then, is someone who feels and reacts to the pain again and again.

Resentment is the opposite of forgiveness. Forgiveness is restorative; it is therapeutic. Forgiveness takes the lopsided scales and puts them right again; it doesn't allow for the holding of grudges or for retaliatory gestures. It isn't compatible with the resentment that encourages a person to live with unequal scales—that is, with disorder and imbalance.

If I forgive, I will have to surrender my grudges, the axes I have to grind with you, the scores I want to settle, and the feelings I enjoy of being superior to you who committed a fault against me. Not only that, but I will have to wish you well, to boot. For the non-forgiver, as for Jonah, this is too much to handle. For the non-forgiver it is easier to curse than to bless.

People Don't Forgive Because of Revenge

Many people don't forgive because of their allegiance to one "principle" or another. These principles are frequently phrased in the form of aphorisms, like:

"I can't let him off too easily," "She's only getting what she asked for," "She doesn't deserve to be forgiven," "I can't be too soft on him," "This will teach him a lesson."

The thread that runs consistently through these aphorisms is *revenge*. Like Jonah, non-forgivers insist that they alone know how to deal with offenders. Even if God intrudes, His suggestions are regarded as naive. The non-forgiver is horrified at thoughts of mercy and compassion at a time when he or she knows how effective revenge will be. So effective, the non-forgiver believes, that the offense will never be repeated. "Let me see her steal again after I cut off her hands," "Let me see her cut class again after I mark her down a grade for the course," "Let me see him come in late again after I take the car keys away forever."

Unfortunately the non-forgiver fails to reflect upon the times he or she has stood in need of mercy and kindness and received them: the considerateness offered when the "book" called for rigidity; the "spirit" when the rules called for the "letter" of the law; flexibility, kindness, forgiveness when there was also punishment and strictness that could have been called into play.

Apart from this amnesia, the non-forgiver perceives revenge as exacting a price for the wrong done. It cancels the debt that he or she calculates is due for the pain incurred. Revenge, then, is guised as "justice," eye-for-an-eye-style, and the non-forgiver can feel strangely comforted by demanding the "pound of flesh."

People Don't Forgive Because It's Socially Unacceptable

This might appear to be a strange way to process forgiveness, but in fact it is very common for people not to forgive because it is not socially acceptable to do so. There are always groups of persons who fall beyond the pale of the restorative practice of forgiveness. Persons who are not dealt with forgivingly are dealt with punitively. Once we deal punitively, we cancel the possibility for forgiveness.

Our prison system, as everyone knows, operates within the punitive model—not the forgiving model of "rehabilitation, restoration, and reintegration into society," and maybe that's why so few of these things ever get done. Convicts never know forgiveness; instead—if they are lucky—they may know conditional pardons and paroles. In fact, "capital punishment," wrote Martin Luther King, Jr., may be considered "society's final assertion that it will not forgive."[3]

Within that context, the governor of the state of New York bore the brunt of severe criticism when he pardoned a terminally ill convicted murderer in the summer of 1978 so that the prisoner could spend his last days at home with his family.[4] A New York state senator vehemently denounced the governor as having been soft on crime, too lenient, and one who obviously did not understand that as much as one might want to be compassionate in such cases, compassion was clearly unwarranted and inappropriate. Criminals would always be criminals, subject to a rigid legal code and not to humanitarian movements of the heart.

Surely common sense would direct us to remove persons of violent, antisocial, or criminal behavior from the orbit of ordinary social intercourse, yet what they are removed to and what processes the system subjects them to become a major concern for us all. It costs the prison system more per year to maintain an inmate in the state of New York than it would to send a man to Harvard.[5] And neither the people of New York nor the Bureau of Prisons is satisfied with its investment.

There are some—those stricken by Ninevitis, a disability that suggests that some are not worthy to be saved—who would consider prisoners and ex-convicts to fall within that purview, to be beyond consideration as brothers and sisters, never to be allowed into the mainstream of American life or into God's forgiving love.

One of the most poignant illustrations of socially conditioned forgiveness, thus non-forgiveness, is told by Alex Haley in *Roots*.[6] Kunta Kinte's daughter Kizzy had been living a reasonably contented life on Massa Waller's plantation when a young male slave escaped. Eventually the runaway is captured and under torture reveals that Kizzy was responsible for the forgery of a traveling document that made his escape initially possible.

Massa Waller, whom we are led to believe is a Christian—church-going and God-fearing—is importuned by Kizzy's mother and father for clemency, for leniency—for forgiveness. They ask Waller to remember their loyalty, they ask to be punished in her place—but to no avail. The social code does not allow slaveowner to forgive slave. The social stratification does not allow Master to be moved by the entreaties of the parents of this young woman. The social code reinforces a punitive reckoning. For this offense, this penalty: Kizzy is summarily sold to another slaveowner and separated from her parents for life.

Kizzy's story haunts me because I have found it repeated in innumerable situations where one person is visibly an authority figure and feels powerless in bending the punitive code because of what people would say or what it would look like.

So, teachers punish students, in moments of anger and frustration, with nonsensical assignments, and then feel powerless to rescind their punishment lest they appear indecisive and weak. And parents follow through on unjust threats because to show compassion and to offer forgiveness, they feel, would be to expose their uncertainties, and they cannot bear that disclosure. And Ninevitis sets in.

Whom is it out-of-fashion to forgive? The list varies, of course.

In the time of Jesus, the hard line was obviously encouraged against tax collectors and prostitutes. Nowadays tax collectors and prostitutes aren't as vulnerable as welfare cheats, dope pushers, abortionists, environmental polluters, sexual deviants, and child abusers. The temperament of a society varies widely in its empathy toward the outcasts of the moment.

And the hard question is this: Suppose God were to give a second chance to these enemies, just as the potter in the Book of Jeremiah[7] who doesn't throw away the clay that has come out misshapen, but puts it back on the wheel and refashions it?

The forgiver insists that this is not letting them off easily ... that forgiveness is ultimately creative ... that it is better to turn the enemy into a friend ... and that it is ultimately a triumph to see Nineveh changed in its heart rather than to see it destroyed!

And we? Would we agree?

People Don't Forgive Because There's an Easier Way

Another reason why people don't forgive is that they fail to see the interconnectedness of the human situation. Baron von Hügel, a gentle and sensible guide in these matters, once wrote to his niece, "I wonder whether you realize a deep great fact? That souls—all human souls— are deeply interconnected?"[8] It takes a wise and discerning person to appreciate the way everyone is dependent on each other—a vision the non-forgiver is blind to.

The non-forgiver is facilitated in this effort at obscurity by what I call a "scissors" mentality to relationships. Through this scissors approach, we are able to cut out of our lives those persons who offend or criticize or are in our disfavor, thereby avoiding or negating the dependency theory. The question of forgiving these persons becomes a moot point, since, very simply, I do not have to forgive someone who has been excised from my life, because for all intents and purposes that person does not exist! I have rendered that person nonexistent!

Forgiveness assumes that we are all members of one family, and that within that family we are all brothers and sisters *in via,* "on the road" to wholeness. The scissors approach to life allows me to admit some persons into the orbit of relationships and to eliminate others. My world then is never "received," but carefully guarded, protected, and chosen.

A friend of mine described to me the situation she confronts on her job, which is revealing in terms of this scissors approach to life. My friend's employer is another woman, a person of modest talent and immodest ambition who regularly chooses to dismiss from her employ anyone who disagrees or insinuates disagreement with her. In some cases it seems that she simply settles for making life unpleasant for the offenders; in most cases, rather than be bothered with even this inconvenience, she settles for the ax—or the scissors—as the metaphor strikes.

There have been some instances in this situation where employees failed the employer: reports not submitted and prepared on time; computational errors undetected until time and patience were lost. In these and other situations the employer chose not to deal with the failures of the subordinates, not to accept their apologies, not to set the balance scales aright—in short, not to forgive. She decided instead on exercising her special prerogative as an "authority" and "superior" to dismiss the offender and thereby remove the culprit from her purview, rather than to deal with the failure from either or both the objective and subjective points of view.

This maneuver, then, becomes a common form of assistance in non-forgiving. When we are able to perceive people as nonpeople, as objects who don't matter, then we don't have to worry about forgiving. This strategy allows us not to deal with hurt and pain because we're moving away from those feelings.

The removal of pain is a central part of the forgiving

process; the forgiver, as we will discuss in Chapter 5, is always conscious of initially relieving pain, and forgiveness is, ultimately, the act that lessens pain and brings soothing peace.

In the scissors mentality, analogously, what I am doing is not lessening pain, but drugging myself so that I don't feel anything. To be sure, there is no pain, but there is dwindling consciousness, too; and there is a distressing reinforcement of a decision to refuse to work through relationships and to grow through that struggle.

Mature people are those who work through relationships. In fact, people who are mature are characterized precisely by their ability to go out to others and get along with others. When there are differences of opinion and perspective, mature people work through these differences. They are flexible, adaptable, and possessed of sufficient emotional stability that they are not burdened by unrealistic threats to their beings from others.

In general, don't we consider the young bride who goes rushing home to her mother after her first argument with her spouse, or the person who crumbles on the job after the first brush with criticism, as immature? People with any sense of the interrelatedness of us all, know the value and importance attached to working things out because we owe it to ourselves as well as to others. Those who do otherwise—people who use scissors to cut out those who don't agree with them—turn out to be very lonely people indeed, and tragically unloving ones, too.

Some years ago I met a family very proficient in the use of scissors, and they considered me at one point their friend. The family consisted of the two parents and their three daughters. The friends of each family member were

24

under constant scrutiny to determine whether they measured up to the standards imposed by mother and father. One slip—failing to include the three sisters in a birthday celebration, or not greeting the parents with beaming smiles and obsequious courtesy—resulted in ostracism from the narrow circle of "friends." One year the parents gave the same Christmas gift to each of the daughters' teachers, to the pastor of the church, and to the principal of the school. Anyone who did not respond immediately with profuse gratitude was eliminated from the list for the next time. Snip.

Eventually I, too, was scissored out of their lives. I never knew for sure why, but I knew enough to recognize that once I was snipped away there was no hope of my being sewn into their lives again.

Last year the mother of the family died. Weeks later I learned from the clergymen who officiated at the service that the father and daughters, expecting large crowds to gather to say their final farewells, enlisted the assistance of the local police to handle traffic on the morning of the funeral. Telegrams were sent to neighbors who had moved away, phone calls were made, and local motels were alerted to prepare for out-of-town guests the night before the burial. Yet in the end, only the husband, the daughters, their husbands, and a grandchild or two attended the services.

People who use scissors in their relationships think they're cutting people out of their lives, while in reality they are cutting themselves out of the human family. Thus, they are people who not only die alone, but whether they know it or not, they live alone as well.

People Don't Forgive Because of Pride

People don't forgive when they have something to lose. Especially when that something is pride.

In the early days of Christianity, when John Cassian listed the seven deadly sins, he suggested that pride belonged at the top of the list because pride subsumed all the rest.[9]

Here, too, while we list pride last of all in the reasons that people don't forgive, it nevertheless looms large over all the other reasons, and in fact sheds light on each of them.

It is pride, in the first place, a pride in the image I have of myself as a lovable, likable, and irresistible person, that doesn't allow me to admit that someone disliked me enough to hurt me; that someone wasn't swept up into the charm that I imagine I exude continually. Because my pride has been so offended, I may choose to deny the pain or to make excuses for my adversary, because to do otherwise would be to admit that I was vulnerable and that someone scratched and exposed that vulnerability.

Have you shared with me the experience of rushing to console a friend who has just been fired? Our friend says, with apparent sincerity, "She didn't fire me. I quit." When we are absolutely sure of our facts, we can accurately surmise the psychological dynamics. Our friend might well be saying, "I didn't want you to know how hurt I am, how vulnerable I am, how embarrassed I am. I didn't want your pity because the image I have of myself is one of unqualified success in all my relationships."

"He didn't throw me out. I left."

"She didn't fail me. I withdrew from the course."

"I wasn't asked to be the leader because he knew I wasn't feeling well."

Pride helps me make all the excuses so that I continue to look good—even if that looking good is only to myself. Everyone around me may in fact know the truth, but in deference to me and my feelings they have to pretend that it is otherwise: "Don't offer him help—his pride will be hurt."

If pride keeps me from admitting the hurt, it surely keeps me from acknowledging that forgiveness is in order and that I'm responsible for coming to terms with it. How can I forgive someone when I haven't admitted that they've affected me?

There is still another prong to the pride issue and it has to do with looking foolish when we forgive. A student of mine once titled a final paper "Are Forgivers Suckers?" and I was both amused and chastened at the aptness of the human predicament she had opened to scrutiny.

In some ways it appears as though the forgiver is precisely that: a fool, a dunce, and certainly one of the world's most unsophisticated creatures—who apparently doesn't realize that in our eager, competitive society, forgiveness gives an advantage to the opposition because it declares the score even and all bets off for a mouth-watering retaliation.

Rather than have one's image enhanced by forgiveness, often enough the opposite happens: our image is eroded so that we look like country bumpkins, unable to handle ourselves in larger and wider social structures, and capable, at any moment, of allowing someone to pull the wool over our eyes. A declaration of forgiveness to our enemies frequently appears as naive and the height of weak and often nonsensical behavior.

Consider along with me the following situation. A woman owed her uncle a large sum of money. After numerous entreaties for payment, the uncle sued. Then the niece countersued, and the war was on. Family members were enlisted to take sides and the community at large was in on the dispute. When the niece realized that she had exhausted her resources and that the legal process would declare her (in all fairness, I might add) responsible for the debt, she went to her uncle, explained her distressing financial picture that was compounded by personal difficulties, and implored his leniency. The uncle forgave the debt and withdrew the lawsuit.

A close observer remarked, "I bet she didn't owe him any money in the first place or he would have pursued the lawsuit. The fact that he withdrew it (and forgave) 'proves' *she* must have been right all along."

What a fascinating thinking process!

If you tell lies about me and I forgive you, you must have been correct in your judgments.

If we're in an argument and I'm the first to apologize, I did it because I knew I was wrong.

This kind of interpretation of our behavior also plays into the image we have of ourselves. Unless we are willing to be misunderstood, our pride will keep us from forgiving, because we are not especially flattered by anyone assuming that our capitulation is actually an avowal of failure and weakness.

Perhaps all of this can be clarified by remembering that forgiveness is a costly business. The pride in us begs for our act of kindness to be recognized and touted from the housetops. "No one finds it simple," wrote Alan Webster, "to bury the hatchet and not to make a virtue of burying it, still less to refrain from marking the place in the ground."[10] Yet forgiveness asks for no memorials. The forgiver looks beyond what others will say to what is true, and one of the things that happens in forgiveness is that a fresh and rarefied form of love is exercised—one whose reward far exceeds the praise of those who do not or cannot understand.

CHAPTER III

What Happens
When People Don't
Forgive

HERE'S a will on file in the Surrogate's Court in Westchester County, New York, that tells us all we may need to know about what happens when people don't forgive.

In the summer of 1977, a five-million-dollar estate was willed in varying portions to a college library, a state museum, a New England finishing school, a medical dispensary, a long-time family chauffeur, and a Methodist church. The only surviving daughter of the deceased woman, a married, middle-aged daughter (and a college classmate of mine), was willed nothing.

The exclusion from the will wasn't a surprise to the daughter; at least, not totally. Ten years before the mother's death, in the middle of an acerbic and protracted family argument, the daughter commiserated with her two aunts, the mother's sisters, who represented the opposing point of view in the family feud.

The details of the argument and the merits of each side are not very important, and so will be omitted here. Let it be said, simply, that both mother and daughter perceived the issues and solutions differently, but while the daughter was able to live within the tension of disagreement with her mother, the mother interpreted the daughter's independent vote as "defiance" and "betrayal." Deeply angered, the mother regarded the daughter's behavior as something she was unable to forgive, and she vowed that someday the daughter would pay for "taking sides" against her.

To effect the punishment, the mother wasted no time in alerting other members of the family of her displeasure at the daughter's injudicious action. She burned the daughter's pictures, refused her telephone calls, and returned her letters unopened. In hurt and anger, she continued to widen the gulf between them—a chasm that the daughter and family members tried unsuccessfully to bridge. The final gesture, executed with elaborate attention to legal detail, involved excluding the daughter from the will.

For the mother, there was no alternative, no compromising the retaliation she had devoted herself to with such determination and passion. The thought that was particularly loathsome to the mother was bequeathing a life of comfort and luxury to someone who had inflicted on her such embarrassment and pain. Presumably an inheritance through the will would have accomplished just that and had to be avoided at any cost.

Some might judge that cost to be excessive, since the

mother spent the last ten years of her life, until she died at sixty-eight, vigorously campaigning against a reconciliation. There are those who say that, at the end, she was more adamantly resolved than ever not to forgive, so that she could wreak her final stroke of retaliation from the grave.

What happens when people don't forgive? Several things, all of them unpleasant and unhealthy.

The story above suggests ten probabilities, and we will content ourselves for the time being with that number, listing them first and elaborating on them later.

When people don't forgive—

(1) They are led by their anger, pain, or hatred;
(2) They are directed by negative memories;
(3) They do not act freely;
(4) They keep a controlling grasp on situations and people;
(5) They are pressured by lives of tension and stress;
(6) They probably shorten their lives;
(7) Their relationships with others are strained;
(8) Their relationship with God is weakened;
(9) They live with feelings of little self-worth;
(10) They feel unrelieved guilt.

When People Don't Forgive They Are Led by Their Anger, Pain, or Hatred

Let's start at the beginning. The first thing that happens when people don't forgive is what this story preeminently illustrates: the non-forgiver decides to be led by anger, pain, or hatred—all three, or any combination.

That decision may be something of a reflex action at first, like flinching before the next blow, but in time the non-forgiver chooses—deliberately decides—to be led by these emotions on a continuing basis.

When a woman lives through a bitter divorce, for example, she may exercise great caution in believing another man's avowal of his love for her. If her experience of rejection is strong enough, her "flinching" reaction to a new suitor's advances might be to deny their sincerity or their depth. Here she's being led by her previous painful experience. She might be thinking, "It's easier to end this relationship now before I get involved, because if I do get involved, you may withdraw your love and I will be rejected once again."

In the period of time immediately following the divorce, this kind of reflex reaction is common and understandable. After a while, this woman faces a more serious set of options: to continue to be led by the pain of rejection, thereby not allowing the possibility of another relationship to develop; or, to work through that fear of rejection—admitting it, confronting it, investigating it, and integrating it—and thereby freeing herself from its grip.

The mother with the five-million-dollar estate faced the same set of options that the divorcée did: she could allow the anger and pain that she once experienced to be replayed every time the memory button was pressed; or, she could come to terms with the pain and its cause and the anger and its cause, and make peace with these tyrannical emotions so that she might be able to make freer choices in the future.

From the evidence we have, it would appear that the mother wasn't too interested in taking the second option with any degree of seriousness. And so she decided with cold deliberateness to be led by the original anger and pain she experienced.

The problem with being led by anger is that anger is a potentially destructive emotion, and it is capable of corroding a person's spirit. Anger unleashed can be cruel, but anger that is allowed to bubble and churn inside us feeds on our insides and debilitates and weakens us. Someone once remarked that emotions are always buried alive, not dead, and because they are living, they are like parasites eating away at our very beings. Being led by these destructive forces incapacitates more than our stomachs.

On one level, of course, we are all led by negative experiences. For me, it only takes one haircut that makes me look like I went through a meat grinder to convince me never to return to the same place and try again. The same if I endure one dreadful TV pilot at the beginning of the season; I will faithfully avoid watching all subsequent episodes. And if a new frozen-food product is a flop with my family, there's no hope for a repeat purchase from us, even if the manufacturer plasters "new" and "improved" on subsequent labels.

Relationships, however, are different from haircuts, television shows, and packaged foods. Relationships involve human lives that beg to be reverenced through commitments and promises, and that require a flexibility on our part to want to iron out differences ... to build bridges ... to mend and amend.

The mender says, "You are important enough for me to give this another try. The only thing I have to lose if my effort at peacemaking fails is a bruised ego, but at least I will have *tried*."

It has to be a sign of strength (and not of weakness) to hold out a hand readily for a handshake with our opponents, and to say, "I'm sorry," or, "Of course, I forgive you," and in that spirit of building and mending and growing, it has to be part of generativity and creativity as well. To choose the opposite—to be led by the pain—may be an inevitable consequence of non-forgiveness, but it is also destructive to the human spirit and ultimately nonproductive for the spirit and nonspirit alike.

Several summers ago we vacationed with a family whose teen-age son was responsible for losing his family's five passports. It was an unfortunate episode. The son stuffed the passports into a plastic shopping bag. On one of our lengthy sightseeing days, in an effort to compress many bulging packages into one, he accidentally discarded the bag with the valued contents.

The loss caused the family (and us) ample inconvenience, but our real dose of suffering came when the boy's father wouldn't drop the episode, wouldn't pick up the pieces and live on. Instead, his anger flared out against the son almost irrationally at the least provocation. Once the father bolted over a table in a restaurant to retrieve a luncheon bill that the son was presenting to the cashier to be paid.

"Let me have that bill," he screamed, "before you lose that, too!"

On another occasion the father tore a road map out of the son's hands, snapping, "I can't trust you with anything!"

"Who asked for your comments? You're too stupid to have an opinion about anything except how to lose things." And on it went.

I thought then (and I think now) of C.S. Lewis's devastating comments in *The Four Loves* on how bitterly cruel parents can be to their children. According to Lewis, the frequent location of adult put-downs is at the dinner table, where the grown-ups can treat children's comments with mockery and disdain.[1] My heart always aches in these situations for both the child, whose feelings are being shattered, and the adult, whose insensitivity destroys the spontaneity and innocence of young people.

To lessen my own ache, and the aches of others on our trip, I did what I could do to de-escalate the anger that the father bore toward the son. My efforts paled in comparison to the gentle voice of reason of the wife-mother. A veteran diplomat could not have been more persuasive than she, yet what she did apparently was not enough because the father railed on. And on. For the entire remaining week of our trip, we were constantly reminded that the child "failed" him, was "irresponsible," "careless," and, "damn it, this time" he was not going to forgive his "bungling and incompetent son." That being decided, there was no alternative other than for the father to be led by his anger, and for the rest of us to learn to handle this miserable situation!

Finally, to add the obvious to this first observation about what happens when people don't forgive: When people don't forgive, they choose to be led by their anger or pain or hatred—*and someone other than the non-forgiver always suffers.*

When People Don't Forgive They Are Directed by Negative Memories

Remember the song "Memories Are Made of This"? Memories are made of today's experiences.[2] What we are living through today becomes tomorrow's memory. Memories, then, are very powerful because they are playbacks of our experiences, our lives. A series of bad experiences as a child becomes a series of bad memories later on and frequently takes professional intervention to heal. Yet, unless these negative memories are healed in prayer or in therapy, they can lead us and direct us and keep us in a kind of bondage.

In the six years that I taught young girls in high school I can recall that many of them lived through dreadful first dates and prom dates and vowed to me through their memory of these evenings that they would never, absolutely never, date another boy again—a promise usually kept for about a week.

Once in a while, though, there was a special case: a young girl who suffered a humiliation significant enough to support and encourage her resolution not to date again, and to keep that promise for a long time.

How powerful memories are!

Unless we are comforted and strengthened when we bring up painful memories, they just don't go away. Or at least they don't go away quickly. I don't think there's a high-school teacher or guidance counselor or parent of teen-agers who doesn't know the value of understanding and love in helping to ease the pain of bad memories. I found this often among my high-school, college, and graduate students. I find this truth lived out now among all people—adults as well as children. We all have a need for painful memories to be healed, because to leave them unhealed is to allow them a powerful directing force in our lives.

I am impressed, frequently and enormously, with the healing of memories that takes place in many of the prayer groups I know.[3] As a process, the healing of the memories involves the willingness to touch base with painful past experiences in our lives so that these experiences will no longer haunt and threaten, but instead will be made whole. Sometimes these experiences are clearly articulated.

"My father never had time for me when I was a little boy. I remember one birthday, he gave me a baseball glove, but wouldn't teach me how to use it. Another time, he gave me a fishing rod, but wouldn't take me fishing. I still feel resentment over my dad's indifference and neglect. I want to forgive him, but I can't!"

Sometimes we feel a general uneasiness about a person or a period in our lives. At such a time the prayer asks for bringing from unconsciousness to consciousness the place where healing is needed. Conscious or subconscious hurts are then exposed to the support of religious faith, where Jesus is asked to be present with us as companion and friend as we confront these painful times of the past. We relive those negative memories with a strength greater than our own and we lean on that power to free us from our old fears and hurtful feelings. These are then exposed and drawn out of an experience, and a confidence and freedom born of our attachment to Christ's spirit takes its place.

I have been privileged at these healing services to see the beginning of an unburdening experience take place. Afterwards I have seen the process continue. People emerge from this experience as different men and women, capable of relating to others and to themselves in a new and freer way.

When people don't forgive they don't forget, and when people don't forget they allow their memories to control them. For non-forgivers, those memories are negative and painful ones. To wit, the five-million-dollar will.

For the mother in that story, her strong, unyielding memory wouldn't loosen its grip on a painful experience. To her dying day her memory of that "betrayal" directed her actions, her desires, and to some degree the future of a daughter she was bound, by hook or by crook, to get even with. By the time I met the mother she was already advanced into a terminal illness, but I speculated then, and had those speculations supported by one of her physicians, that the compulsive devotion she exercised toward her revenge most probably exacerbated (if it did not outright cause) her illness. More about that later.

For now, let's look at the stories about the will and the lost passports as stories where we find characters who were led by negative memories. One mother and one father were unable to look at their children and say, "You hurt me terribly. You didn't measure up to what I wanted of you *that time*—in *that experience*—so one or two or even ten of my memories of you aren't good ones." But there are other memories—good memories—to balance with the bad memories, and in the balance we owe it to each other not to be led by the bad ones. The parents in these stories were unable to make this kind of judgment and instead allowed the hostile memories to live on unabated.

When People Don't Forgive They Do Not Act Freely

Sometimes, of course, there are no good memories to reckon with. Stories that people have told us about their experiences in concentration camps, prisons, and orphanages, and even within families, are often enough, and tragically, only negative.

What then? Even then, I believe, we don't have to be led by these bad memories. Even then, we can reach for a power and a force greater than those memories to direct us and to lead us. Viktor Frankl, the founder of logotherapy, tells us that he was able to live through the horror of the Nazi concentration camp at Dachau because of his will to find meaning in the experience.[4] Somewhere in all of the suffering and pain there had to be a purpose, and the search for that meaning is what kept him alive. Evangelist Corrie ten Boom writes of her experience in another concentration camp that what kept her and her sister Betsie going was the sense of mission to return and tell anyone who would listen that the human spirit is indomitable and can survive if it keeps faith in God.[5]

The alternative to finding that faith or meaning, either of which constitutes a power of equal or greater strength than the painful memory, is to be guided, directed, and led by the memory—which, in turn, means that we are not acting freely.

Why we bother at all to find something stronger than the anger or pain to lead us is in great measure because of our awareness of the lives of those who have acted freely in the most impossible of circumstances. These people speak of seeing with new eyes, of being released from bonds that held them back, of a fuller taste of peace, so that they are able to live far more abundantly than the meager measure they might have settled for.

The testimony of those led by pain, on the other hand, is a chronicle of depressing and tortured self-pity and unhappiness—hardly an attractive option.

Remember the story about the man who rides the bus to work each morning? Each day he is met by a sour, embittered bus driver who has only gruff words to offer his passenger.

"Why," a friend of the passenger asks, "do you put up with his rudeness? Why are you always so courteous and gracious when this man insists on insulting you?"

"Because," replies the passenger, "I refuse to let this man dictate to me how I'm going to act."

The passenger on the bus is a person who refuses to be programmed by someone else's behavior. This is the story of a person who chooses to act freely. In many ways it parallels stories of prisoners who have maintained their own dignity in the most degrading of circumstances. Sometimes these prisoners have even "won over" their guards by their kindness and patience.[6] It is another way of saying what Paul wrote in his Captivity Epistles: You do not hold the keys to anything that can chain my spirit. My spirit remains free no matter what you do to me![7] Perhaps that's all that has to be said here: Even when there are no positive memories to take into account, we need not be led by our painful ones. Even then it is possible to seek out and to find enough will or strength to avoid being held in crippling servitude. To be free!

When People Don't Forgive They Keep a Controlling Grasp on Situations and People

Possibly a picture comes to mind—a picture of a person with clenched fists, shaking them at the world, never loosening the fingers, never opening them, never letting go. A lot of energy gets used up in this heroic effort of controlling. The mother with her five million dollars tried to do it with her money and her daughter: Keep them grasped tightly; control them. All non-forgivers do it one way or another.

Non-forgivers choose to focus on themselves—their

own pain and hurts. Their feelings come first, last, and in the middle, too. They move deeper and deeper into selfish, egotistical behavior patterns, and the tightfisted grasp is an image of what that self-centered pattern of acting looks like. It isn't relaxed, it isn't open, free, and vulnerable. "This image of the tightly clenched fist shows the tension, the desire to cling tightly to yourself, a greediness which betrays fear," writes Henri Nouwen, a native-Dutch pastoral theologian currently at Yale.[8]

Even though our mother willed her five million dollars to worthwhile causes, her gifts, as Paul suggests, were without the authentic ring of love. Her largesse to her charities in no way redeemed the pettiness that consumed her heart.

We are aware, thanks to the work of Alfred Adler, of the role that compensation plays in the psychological makeup of a person.[9] Adler noticed, initially, that when a physiological organ is lacking or removed, other organs obligingly take its place. One kidney, for example, takes over for both when the other kidney is dysfunctional. And the blind person seeks to compensate for blindness by heightening the senses of touch and hearing. This model from the physiological sphere threw light on certain psychological areas.

As a psychological phenomenon, compensation is an ego defense through which a person will resort to diversionary tactics by substituting quantity for quality. Thus, people overdevelop certain conscious elements as a defense against unconscious tendencies of unappealing character that threaten to come into consciousness.

In this kind of "reaction formation," we can find a small boy (and children are helpfully transparent in this regard) reacting against feelings of jealousy and hostility toward his little sister by showing unusually solicitous concern for her. It is almost as if his behavior were saying, "Before someone detects my true feelings, or even before my true feelings come to the surface, I will give evidence of the opposing feelings, and the outside world (and even I) may never suspect what's really going on."

The Gospel is aware of this kind of compensating activity when it calls to task those who do the seemingly praiseworthy business of giving gifts on the altar but are at odds with their brothers and sisters in the bargain (Matt. 5:23). These are the persons who are severely censured. "Go first and be reconciled!" Or, go first and give your money to your families (who may not pin medals on you or elect you to office), before you give your gifts elsewhere for attention and fanfare.

The attempt to stifle guilt feelings through some good action, as our wealthy woman tried to do through her will, didn't erase the egocentricity at the depths of her being. All it did was to sidetrack us for a while.

In the end, after the dust settled, she was recognized as selfish—and not only selfish, but probably tired as well. Exercising control over situations and people's lives can take a lot out of anyone. Think of the consciousness you'd have to exercise *constantly*, being watchful and on guard that your heart would not be moved, that your emotions would not be changed, that war instead of peace would triumph.

I am sometimes amused, mostly saddened, and often amazed at the intricate and elaborate curses that people place over others' lives. This is another way of controlling the future, of keeping that grasp on people and events as tightly as one can, and these curses are a way of saying, "Just in case I fail at my plot for revenge, I trust that there will be other people—your children, your employees—who will do to you what you did to me or punish you by giving you heartache and pain." In the end, the one who curses even asks God, the devil, or other transcendent powers, to be in cahoots with him or her to cause the other person not to be forgiven; to cause some form of excruciating suffering in payment.

The grip of the non-forgiver is a vise, a muscular tour de force, that concentrates every moment and every movement on retaliation.

When People Don't Forgive They Are Pressured by Lives of Tension and Stress

For those who forgive as well as for those who do not, life has to go on—children have to be fed, jobs have to be attended to, bills have to be paid. Beneath all of this the non-forgiver has another agenda percolating. The non-forgiver is on the lookout for the right moment to counterattack, to get revenge.

There is never a moment of peace for the non-forgiver. Non-forgivers are always on their toes, ready to pounce on their prey, ready to attack or to arrange for someone else to even the score. That kind of game-planning is, minimally, what we could call stressful living.

An employer who unjustly fired one of his employees several years ago still follows the career of his ex-employee with fanatical zeal. Wherever he can, the former employer feels duty bound to say a few negative words to discourage other employers from hiring the young man, and he schedules meetings and social events according to their possibility of placing him in touch with persons with whom he can do the most harm to his former employee.

Why? Maybe because he can't forgive the young man's talents and abilities.

Maybe because he can't forgive his own poor judgment in firing him.

Maybe because he can't forgive the consequences of his own jealous rage.

The stress is further exacerbated by the non-forgiver's need to camouflage these feelings of rage in front of others, or, just the opposite, to maintain a semblance of fury at all times. Either way, it's stressful business.

It could also be that the non-forgiver has no place to let off steam, to expose his or her uncertainties about this tension-filled game plan, to seek help in order to alter strategies. The non-forgiver, then, is all alone acting out this scheme for revenge, willfully or not, pressured on all sides and not able to see a way out.

When People Don't Forgive They Probably Shorten Their Lives

Stressful living, of course, can have serious physical as well as psychological ramifications. We are all one piece— body, spirit, and psyche—and when one part is injured, chances are we can look for some effect every place else.

Several years ago Drs. Friedman and Rosenmann published an interesting study of two behavioral types of people.[10] They classified these persons as Type A and Type B. The Type A persons were overachievers, always occupied, burning the candle at both ends: aggressive, stress-filled, and tense. Type B persons were mañana people, those who could wait, exercise patience, deliberate, consider; they were less fretful and "hyper" than their brothers and sisters in the Type A group.

Friedman and Rosenmann established a strong causal relationship between Type A persons and those who were prone to heart attacks. Since we can establish an even stronger connection between the consequences of non-forgiveness and some of the characteristics of Type A persons, an interesting syllogism emerges.

(1) People who live stressful and tension-filled lives are prone to heart attacks.
(2) Non-forgivers live stressful and tension-filled lives. Therefore,
(3) Non-forgivers are prone to heart attacks. Who knows?

In a related area, Dr. O. Carl Simonton and Dr. Stephanie Simonton suggest in their research that stressful emotional states make people more susceptible to cancer.[11] The Simontons maintain that there are four characteristics found among those prone to cancer:

(1) A poor self-image;
(2) An inadequate ability to form long-term relationships as well as to maintain them;
(3) A prevalence toward self-pity;
(4) A tendency to hold resentment which involved a sustained inability to forgive.

While the research of these medical teams is in some ways inconclusive, it has the certain ring of common sense about it. It's hard to imagine that a person is psychologically a wreck and that this disability isn't affecting the body adversely as well. Minimally it would seem plausible to expect a state of exhaustion resulting from the manipulation and strategizing that goes on in effecting revenge. Minimally. And quite possibly a lot more damage is heaped on the body in the course of the campaign to retaliate.

Can it really be disputed that one of the things that happens when people don't forgive is that, in not loosening their grip on things, they remain in a tension that gnarls the body as well as the psyche, and causes damage to both? I doubt it.

When People Don't Forgive Their Relationships with Others Are Strained

What probably needs saying at the outset, in a sort of umbrella way, is that non-forgiveness affects all of our relationships adversely. Non-forgiveness, after all, negates relationships. To talk about "non-forgiveness" and in the same breath to talk about "relationships,"—be these relationships with God or our friends or even with ourselves—is virtually impossible.

When relationships come into being, a person moves out from within and attends to the other person. The late French existential philosopher Gabriel Marcel talks about two persons in love being present to each other and being available to "serve the promise of each other."[12] In that process lovers see in each other their lovability, and promise to remain faithful to that vision come thick or thin. Lovers, according to Marcel, will also see the negative side of the beloved, but that side will not be served as the promise of the totality of who that person is. The hope is that in serving and reinforcing what is true and beautiful, that part of the personality will flourish.

When relationships come into being, then, a narrow, lonely, selfish, ego-centered world is closed, and a world of communicating the self at the deepest possible level, of sharing, and of growing, is possible.

People who insist on remaining non-forgiving forfeit the possibility for any such meaningful relationship. In the first place—for whatever reason—non-forgivers have abrogated a relationship with the person they've decided they're not going to forgive. That's one relationship off the scoreboard.

But it doesn't stop there. There are always more people involved. For example, in a family setting, if the mother-in-law determines that she's not going to forgive a daughter-in-law for an offense (real or imagined, it doesn't much matter), then it is not only the relationship between these two women which is at stake. Suppose, for example, a third relative asks both the mother-in-law and the daughter-in-law and their spouses to Thanksgiving dinner. The mother-in-law has only two options open to her if she remains non-forgiving: (1) to decline the invitation: "If she's coming, count me out"; or (2) to accept the invitation with conditions spoken or implied: "I'll come but don't expect me to make conversation with her," or "I'll come later and leave early," or even "I'll come but seat us at opposite ends of the table."

We've all been treated to amusing caricatures of this type of encounter. Among the guests at the dinner table, only these two do not speak to each other, and thereby force the other guests to relay their comments for each opponent separately. This turns out to be very exhausting, unpleasant, and unnecessary for the guests. And at its base, it is utterly destructive to community.

It would appear somewhat obvious, then, that relationships with others also suffer. Even for those family members, friends, and acquaintances outside the orbit of the fray, relationships become very difficult for the non-for-giver to maintain. This is due mostly to the non-forgiver's tiring (to us), perduring self-centeredness, which requires a continual rehashing of the disagreement, within which the non-forgiver demands from us a nod of loyal reassurance that he or she is making the right decision. And the relationship is further strained by the joylessness that surrounds these meetings. It's anything but joyful to hear the story of self-centered woe over and over again.

When People Don't Forgive Their Relationship with God Is Weakened

There's another relationship that suffers when we don't forgive, and that's our personal relationship with God.

We hear a great deal about the need for communication in all of our relationships: the need for sharing; the need for taking risks in exposing our deepest selves. Prayer is the way that communication, sharing, and growing takes place between us and God.

Those who are gifted in the articulation of the prayer experience tell us that when authentic prayer is stirring in our hearts, God responds to our avowals of love by extending to us the power of His love in order that we may love our brothers and sisters with Him. There is no prayer, then, that is merely vertical—from us to God and from God to us. All prayer, at the moment of our commitment to God (the vertical dimension), is possessed of a horizontal dimension by the Lord's invitation "to love those He loves."

The fact of the matter is that God's love extends to all,

and this fact is vividly illustrated in the death of Jesus "for all humankind."

The non-forgiver is unable to accept this family context. The non-forgiver is compelled to place conditions on how his or her love will be acted out on the social level.

"I'll love X and Y, but I won't be able to love Z. And I wish, God, that you wouldn't show any special kindness to Z either."

"I'll pray for the welfare of M and N, but I can't ask that you look favorably on O and P."

The Rabbinic Jewish tradition teaches that one must not only come to the aid of one's enemy, but one must pray for that enemy as well.

"If a man has received an injury, then even if the wrongdoer has not asked his forgiveness, the receiver of the injury must nevertheless ask God to show the wrongdoer compassion, even as Abraham prayed to God for Abimelech (Gen. 20:17), and Job prayed for his friends."[13]

This teaching found further expression in the requirement that when a person is called on to lead the congregation in prayer as the Reader of the service, he is obliged to remove all hostility from his heart. He is even asked to explicitly include his enemies in his prayers. In the event that a member of the congregation senses a hostility toward him from the Reader, he may ask the Reader for a specific remembrance in prayer.

Without this kind of open and forgiving attitude, our prayers do not catch fire and ascend to heaven. They remain, instead, smoldering and smoking and very much earthbound.

Without this kind of open and forgiving attitude, there is strain and deceit in our relationship with God. Just as there would be profound pain in a human relationship if we refused to love those dearest to our beloved's heart, so, too, in prayer, the ultimatum "They go or I go" doesn't set a climate conducive to the total engagement that prayer calls for. And the relationship between lover and beloved, or between pray-er and God, can never survive nonnegotiable, unforgiving terms.

Talking about these nonnegotiable terms in prayer is not the same as talking about emotions in prayer. There is always a place for emotions in prayer—even when these emotions are negative. If prayer is a relationship, it should be able to sustain a friendship even when we are feeling hostile or jealous or angry.

Those who wrote the psalms emoted frequently and vehemently; they were obviously free in expressing their emotional states with candor to Yahweh. In the process of this emotional catharsis, though, the singers of these psalms were able to see their feelings transformed by Yahweh, to see their emotional equilibriums shifted, from a desire to avenge their enemies, to a trust in Yahweh. This was not a trust that Yahweh would exact the revenge, but usually a trust that Yahweh would protect the psalmist in future encounters with the enemy.

This kind of letting-go is frequently perceptible in the psalms.[14] We first meet the psalmist in emotional distress. We hear the plea for retaliation and revenge. And then we experience a change taking place: Yahweh enters the picture and defuses the sound and the fury. The psalmist is able to relax and to see the options with some clarity. These options usually boil down to putting all of one's energy in pursuing retaliation with a vengeance—or to placing one's confidence in Yahweh, who will not leave us unprotected against our foes. The psalmist chooses wisely—and Yahweh's hand guides the future.

This posture, as we mentioned earlier, is radically different from the person who at the crucial moment decides to pursue the route of revenge with no holds barred. That decision has mighty consequences in rendering any relationship impoverished.

When People Don't Forgive They Live with Feelings of Little Self-Worth

Non-forgivers live with great dislike and great disesteem for themselves. The unforgiving person says something like, "You're not OK for doing something wrong, and I'm not OK for letting you or what you did get to me. I also may be feeling guilty for not forgiving you, and because all of these things are gnawing at me, I am unhappy. Because I am unhappy, I don't much care to be with myself, and when I am, I don't much like myself. Which brings me back to thinking that I'm not worth very much."

On the surface it may look like the non-forgiver is in control, poised, and self-confident. After all, the unforgiving person appears to be calling all the plays, withholding pardon, maintaining a strict sense of justice—*on the surface.*

We can probably get a more accurate picture of the non-forgiver's inner conflicts by considering the behavior of the bully. The bully seems to have all the confidence in the world when he's pushing around the weaker and feebler. Underneath it all the bully is insecure and threatened, and the aggressiveness and bravado that we see is a shield against vulnerability. So, too, for the non-forgiving person. What we see isn't all that's going on within the person. The inner turmoil is taking a pretty heavy toll.

Self-worth is born in the non-forgiving person just as it

is in the forgiver—when we expose our most vulnerable selves to another and are accepted and loved as we are. When I embrace that acceptance, which is another's statement of my lovability, my self-worth soars. "No self-acceptance is possible," wrote Paul Tillich, "if one is not accepted in a person-to-person relation."[15] The love that someone else has for me is always characterized by self-donation and forgetting the past—not ego gratification or manipulation—and the motivation to seek my happiness and fulfillment. If I choose to accept that love, I will imitate the lover, I will grow in respect of my personhood, and I will increase (or restore) my self-worth. If, on the other hand, I choose not to forgive, I will imitate not the lover but the aggressor.

An implicit contradiction exists between self-donation and aggression, and thus between loving and non-forgiving. Or to put it another way, as long as I remain a non-forgiver, I remain a nonlover, and my self-worth suffers because I am not choosing sides with someone who is affirming my lovability.

Perhaps I have made it appear in these few paragraphs as though someone who does not forgive cannot love—and while I am inclined to believe that this is true a good deal of the time, I must admit that it is certainly true that we can love and hate at the same time. In fact, it is even possible to love and hate the same person!

At the very least, however, it would seem that when we hate we are displacing a great deal of energy that could be channeled into loving, into actions that contradict our loving side. When the spouse of the non-forgiver protests, "I wish you'd forget about him and your vengeance, and love me and let me love you instead," we are treated to a caricature of this situation. In that protestation the lover is witnessing to the fact that loving and non-forgiving are on a collision course and that the resentment and hostility are chipping into and corroding love. My guess is that they chip away at and corrode self-esteem as well.

When People Don't Forgive They Feel Unrelieved Guilt

Let's back up a little. Before we make a connection between non-forgiveness and unrelieved guilt, let's take a look to see where guilt comes from.

Guilt is triggered when we feel we owe somebody something.

So . . . a working mother can feel guilty when she is not baking brownies for her children at two in the afternoon, because she feels she "owes" them this kind of attention. A husband can feel guilty when he doesn't remember his wife's birthday, because he "owes" her a card, a gift, a remembrance.

Where does this "owing" sense come from?

It comes from two places: *my world* (that world that tells me a good mother does this, a good husband does that) and *myself* (that part of me that tells me who I am and encourages my behavior to conform to this image).

I can experience realistic goals set by my world and myself (a mother should feed her family), or I can experience unrealistic goals from my world and myself (a mother should prepare gourmet dinners elegantly served on appliquéd place mats each night).

Failure to measure up to *realistic* goals produces *healthy* guilt. Failure to measure up to *unrealistic* goals produces *neurotic* guilt.

We cope with failure at the realistic goals by admitting the guilt, accepting it, and learning to live by taking it into account in the future. (If I did a poor job on a report because I saved it for the last minute, I can feel guilty. Next time I'll get my act together earlier, get the help I need, and get the report done well and on time.)

Coping with failure at unrealistic goals is a little more difficult. First of all, I'll have to accept limitation—mine or someone else's. It's not especially helpful to live up to an unrealistic image I have of myself or to expect someone else to live up to an unrealistic image I have of him or her. Secondly, I'll have to exchange or reduce the unrealistic goals for realistic ones. Thirdly, I'll have to proceed as above with the realistic, healthy guilt by admitting it and learning from it.

When I refuse to forgive, I claim a triumph for failure—mine or another's. Someone's sin or mistake or error in judgment can lead our lives. Forgiveness, on the other hand (and most importantly), is an invitation to redeem failure. Guilt as a healthy feeling is probably alerting me to a failure somewhere that needs resolving.

There are those who tell us that all guilt is useless and unnecessary. This is simply not so. Guilt as a healthy feeling begs for acknowledgment and resolution through self-forgiveness or by forgiving others their trespasses. To do otherwise is to choose to live without accepting failure as part of life and without growing because of it. It is to live haunted, if not consumed, by a guilt that leaves all my relationships, including the one I have with myself, in a debit column.

CHAPTER IV

Forgiveness

J UST LAST WEEK I learned something about the practice of forgiveness in the Jewish tradition that I had never known before. In a situation where one is called on to help a friend and to help an enemy at the same time, one is obliged to go first to the aid of one's enemy. The Talmud offers two reasons for this unusual behavior. The first reason is to crush the evil *yetzer*, that egocentric, selfish, and aggressive part of the personality which delights in seeing one's enemy miserable. The second reason is to crush the enemy's *yetzer*, thereby enabling him or her to want to become a friend.[1]

All that appears as foolish, outrageous, and even scandalous about the practice of forgiveness is summarized in this short Rabbinic teaching: Love your neighbor even when your neighbor is your enemy; put your enemy's needs ahead of the needs of your friends; and do what you can to secure the friendship of that enemy (to make that enemy *want to be* your friend) for everyone's sake.

The text does not stand alone in the history of religious literature. Just at the point where we might be tempted to dismiss it as fanciful, unrealistic, and unaware of "how people really are," the New Testament offers one of its many examples of the uncommon, forgiving behavior asked of the followers of Jesus Christ. Luke's Gospel (6:27–29) records the following:

When someone slaps you on one cheek, turn and offer the other.

When what is yours is taken, do not demand it back.

Bless those who curse you.

Pray for those who maltreat you.

Pardon and you will be pardoned.

As if this weren't enough, the Gospel (6:30–34) continues: If you choose to do good to those who do good to you, how much effort does that require? Or if you love those who return your love? Or give to those who give to you? Anyone, it seems, can measure up to those standards.

The follower of Jesus is called to give to those who give nothing in return. Love those who do not praise you for your care or reciprocate your love *and* keep that channel of loving open at the cost of whatever pain you can bear, or "deaths" you can endure.

All that's been said about non-forgiveness as common, ordinary, and human comes again into focus. Forgiveness hardly qualifies as any of those things.

What is ordinary is hating our enemies; what is extraordinary is loving them.

What is ordinary is going first to aid our friends; what is extraordinary is going first to aid our enemies.

What is ordinary is feeling good about our enemy's troubles; what is extraordinary is "caring" (a word the root of which means "crying out with the pain and brokenness of another") with sympathy and empathy.

What is ordinary is fumbling in relationships; what is extraordinary is growing within them, enlarging our spirits and the spirits of those around us.

To err is human. And ordinary.

To forgive is extraordinary. And divine. And uncommon—and not instinctive. In fact, forgiveness runs precisely counter to our instincts. It tugs us beyond the place where we would want to declare our pain, nurse our hurts, and invoke sympathy. It encourages us to give more than we planned to give, or thought ourselves able to give.

The fact of the matter is that no one wants to remain where he or she is. Forgiveness awakens us all to that real, though undernourished, part of ourselves that understands our lives as being not as ordinary as we may have thought. Forgiveness talks to us where we are, never deceived about our true condition. Yet it gives us access to our own possibilities in reaching for and making a very unordinary style of life our own.

Forgiveness Is an Empowered Form of Giving

Etymologically, *to forgive* is an extended, expanded, strengthened, and empowered form of the verb *to give*.[2] Experientially it is those things, too.

This is an intriguing suggestion because to be fully alive and fully human is to be a giver; precisely, to be one who gives love. That act of self-donation—"all that I am and all that I have"—appears deceptively simple at first, until the ego-defense mechanisms set in, interfere with the process, and distract us from pursuing a life of selfless love with zeal and single-eyed fidelity. Then we sense resistance even to "giving," and recognize that simple aim as a lifelong task and a graced achievement. The question then boils down to "If *giving* is what it means to be human, what more can "*for*-giving" be?

Forgiving begins where giving ends. Forgiveness assumes that the only gift worth giving is the self, but the condition of the self is different for the giver and for the forgiver. The forgiver is hurt, feels pain, anger, frustration, and hears a call, still, to remain open and giving.

There's a world of difference between what's asked of a giver and a forgiver. For example:

· I have been asked to a party being given for a co-worker. My presence, my time, my donation toward a gift, are all called for and expected. I weigh the time factor (a conflict) and the financial contribution (a strain), but I am anxious to show my co-worker my admiration and esteem and so I am willing to shuffle my agenda and budget and be part of the event.

I am a giver. Now consider the difference between the above and the following:

· I have been asked to a party for a co-worker who betrayed my confidence several years ago. The wounds of the relationship have never healed; confidence and friendship were never restored. I am now asked to contribute my time (which I resent) and my money (the final insult) toward festivities for someone I'm not especially fond of.

Isn't this a bit too much to ask?

· Yet, in the middle of the conflict I see that the party gives me a chance to reexamine and perhaps reintegrate my feelings. On the one hand, I can still admit the fact of the betrayal, and on the other hand, I can consider the party invitation as a gesture toward possible reconciliation. I weigh whether I want that. I decide to stick my neck out and bend toward forgiveness and peace. I'll do my share toward burying the hatchet.

I am a forgiver. The forgiver is asked to put the pain aside (after recognizing it and identifying it), to be other-centered, by looking at the one seeking or in need of forgiveness, and not at his or her own wound. The giver is asked to be generous. The forgiver is asked to be magnanimous and even heroic.

I have heard of cases where victims of rape, burglary, assault, and other crimes have contacted their assailants and extended forgiveness to them. This is one of the touchstones of P.S. Ministries, an offshoot of the Campus Crusade. The work began several years ago by two Christians, a husband and wife, who were robbed at knifepoint in their home. Some time later they wrote their attacker in prison and told him that they had forgiven him. Their letter led to an extended correspondence which eventually led to the conversion of the offender. In the process the couple recognized some of the needs of prisoners as well as the correlation between forgiveness and wholeness, and the P.S. Ministries was formed.

Every age raises up the company of others who witness to the wisdom and benefits of choosing to love even those who hate us. Just at a time when forgiveness seems unnecessary if not totally ludicrous, some one person tries it and shares the results of his or her experiment with great enthusiasm.

Cesar Chavez leaves the courtroom and prepares for jail saying, "Although I think the judge is wrong, I'm not angry."[3] The courage and joy of this man awakens in the crowds of migrant workers the desire to imitate him. The hope and imagination of these people has been stirred by a call for more than better wages and collective bargaining (as valuable as these things are). Their goal is to breathe the air of freedom that this man enjoys. His peacemaking efforts have reaped a harvest greater than lettuce or grapes, and he has given many a glimpse of the things planned for those who live as forgivers.

The fact of the matter is that "forgiveness is the only reaction which does not merely re-act but acts anew and unexpectedly, unconditioned, by the act that provoked it, therefore freeing from its consequence both the one who forgives and the one who is forgiven."[4] It is the surprise element of forgiveness, plus its ability to reverse the direction of the consequences of the initial aggressive action, that enables it to be seen as a most attractive option.

Those who forgive, talk of non-forgiveness as living with death. In the non-forgiving dimension, they surrendered to a grieving process where something had ended: a relationship, a career, health, a secret, a reputation, a dream. Non-forgiveness reinforced the experience of the end, of the void; it was a terrifyingly empty experience without hope.

To move from that experience to the forgiveness dimension was like moving from darkness to light. The forgiveness dimension affirmed that in hope and the power of God our lives are never beyond repair. Non-forgiveness is a way of reaffirming death; forgiveness is a way of reaffirming life.

Forgiveness Is an Invitation

Characteristically, an invitation is "a gift" and cannot be forced. When we "gift" forgiveness, we invite someone to recognize himself or herself as a person of worth and great value. We make a decisive proclamation that someone is worth redeeming, that they are more than this painful thing they did, and we ask them to affirm this about themselves with us.

Andras Angyal, a Boston psychiatrist, explains how this process works by suggesting that forgiveness has both a negative and a positive dimension, implying both a denial and an assertion. Forgiveness has a negative aspect when we face the destructive, unhealthy, ill-motivated behavior head-on, but do not consider this behavior as a measure of what the person is in his or her deepest self. "This negative aspect is a forgiving in the sense of giving away, of removing, unveiling, as if one puts aside a mask which is not organically a part of the person."[5]

The positive aspect of forgiving consists in unmasking, in making apparent the intrinsic value, the genuine worth of the person. The forgiver honors the "offender" as a child of God, never condoning the offense, but always affirming the truth that human nature is basically good since, at the core of our being, Christians profess, is the Holy Spirit.

This is not to deny the reality of sin and the fact that it is possible (and common enough) for us to choose evil. But it is always possible for the lover to separate the sinner from the sin; to continue to love the person and to disapprove the unsound behavior.

For many people, Dr. Angyal tells us, the first experience of a forgiving relationship occurs in therapy between the patient and the therapist. There the therapist's "forgiving" act is not a single, dramatic event but a laborious "translation," item by item, liberating the components of the person's life from their unsound context and salvaging them, in a manner of speaking, by transferring them into healthy structures. The patient notices that the therapist does not blame and does not judge, even though the therapist takes seriously the unwholesome attitudes and behavior of the patient—in some ways, more seriously than the patient himself does because the therapist perceives more clearly their destructiveness. Nevertheless, the therapist continues to value the patient, recognizing in him, beyond all the shortcomings, a likable and worthwhile human being. Because of this translation, the patient is also gradually able to recognize in himself something that is real, but different and apart from his neurotic way of life. That vision provides a fulcrum outside the context of the neurotic enclosure for accepting the invitation to be forgiven and recognizing oneself as of enormous value.[6]

Good parenting and successful friendships provide the same liberating context. When we get right down to it, what we look for in our friendships are people who will accept us and understand us even when our dark side is revealed. To be loved for the good times alone is scarcely the test of any relationship. When we admit our weaknesses, confess our sins, acknowledge our vulnerabilities, we both fear and hope for the consequences. Our fear, of course, is being rejected at the most intimate moment of our self-disclosure. *Why Am I Afraid to Tell You Who I Am?* asks the title of an exceptionally fine book by John Powell.[7] A friend answers him and articulates our common fear: "If I tell you who I am, you may not like who I am, and it is all that I have."

Along with this risky adventure of self-disclosure is the

hope that in spite of my failures there is someone who will understand and love me without judging, without burdening me with little nuggets of advice, who will listen to me and not run away.

The good friend is one who holds me accountable for my talents and my weaknesses, encourages me in my hopes and dreams, and is companion to me when I look into the mirror of the water which "does not flatter" and "faithfully shows whatever looks into it."[8] C.G. Jung promises that "this confrontation is the first test of courage on the inner way, a test sufficient to frighten off most people [because] the meeting with ourselves belongs to the more unpleasant things that can be avoided so long as we can project everything negative into the environment."[9] Only those who love can share that journey with us as we unmask and reveal that which has become part of the fiber of our lives.

In the end it is only the person who loves who can understand the unrestricted nature of forgiveness. Only lovers can understand the behavior of King David when he receives word that his son Absalom—the same son who has waged a fierce war with David—has been brutally killed in battle. At that extraordinary moment, David both loves his son Absalom and forgives his infidelity. In the terror of separation that is part of all grieving, David cries out, "Absalom, O Absalom, would that I could have died in your place!" (2 Sam. 19:1) Which is to say, "Absalom, you are loved and forgiven no matter what you've done, because what you've done is not all there is to you, and, in fact, obscures the image of the Creator stamped on your heart."

"Would that I could take your place!" One way or another, all forgivers invite their foes to the same thing.

David is able to separate the "sinner" from the "sin." He can continue to love, lavishly and profusely, at the same time that he recognizes with precision and clarity Absalom's destructive behavior.

The French Dominican theologian Bernard Bro suggests, in a unique meditative reflection on this scene, the possibility that David never understood the fullness of Yahweh's forgiveness of him until he saw his own capacity to forgive his erring son.[10] It just might have been that David considered himself unworthy of forgiveness, perhaps unforgiven or not forgiven totally. Perhaps he wondered, as we all do, whether there really does exist someone who can forgive so radically that it actually alters the shape of reality. He wonders (and so do we) until he finds himself capable of giving and forgiving in measure he never imagined. "If you can do these things, how much more does your heavenly Father?" (Luke 11:13)

Hannah Arendt puts it this way: "Forgiving and the relationship it establishes is always an eminently personal (though not necessarily individual or private) affair in which *what* was done is forgiven for the sake of *who* did it."[11] If we take the Christian teaching on love with appropriate seriousness, it must be true that only love can forgive. According to Arendt, this is so because "only love is fully receptive to *who* somebody is, to the point of being always willing to forgive him whatever he may have done."[12]

There's still another aspect of this invitation process that can best be understood when we resituate forgiveness in the context of gift. As both gift and invitation, forgiveness needs to be received in order to have the act complete.

Many ask, "Why bother? Why go through this difficult personal process when I know that my forgiveness isn't going to be appreciated or accepted?" There *is*, of course, tremendous value in forgiving even if that act is not accepted. There is great value to the forgiver, who is free from the bondage of a heavy and hardened heart; there is enormous value to the community because of the ripple effect of all of our actions on everyone else. And though it is hard—if not impossible—to perceive, there is benefit to those who stand in need of forgiveness, because we have placed no barrier in the way in the event that they recognize and acknowledge the offense as theirs.

Nevertheless, there are few joys that compare with the completed act of forgiveness offered and forgiveness received. And forgiveness is received when the person in need of forgiveness admits fault or error and turns from it. There are many words for this process. Conversion. Repentance. Metanoia. Contrition. Amendment. And they all point to the same truth: In order to accept the invitation to value myself and to see myself as worthy, I will have to yield that part of me that is the impediment to my actualizing this fullness.

H.R. Mackintosh, a Scottish theologian, says that the process of forgiveness is first owning and then disowning our sins.[13] It is the specific acknowledgment of concrete acts for which we are truly sorry. There is no room for equivocation, no place for vague generalities and disclaimers ("*If* I have been unkind or impatient," "If only *you* weren't so touchy," "*If* I had had more sleep"). That kind of admission simply evades the issue. And the issue is that I am responsible and that I have failed in my responsibility in concrete, specific acts which have to be named, just like a sickness has to be named, because the diagnosis precedes the cure, and healing takes place most efficiently when the diagnosis has been accurate.

"In the naming of the daimonic," writes Rollo May, "there is an obvious and interesting parallel to the power of naming in contemporary medical and psychological therapy."[14] "And then, if I overcome the disease, I shall partly be a new being, and I could rightly be initiated into a new community and be given a new name."[15]

If the first step on the road to becoming a new being, then, is owning the offense, the second step is disowning it—turning it over, surrendering it—placing it in hands which are able to lift our burdens so that we no longer have to carry the weight of their guilt.

I am talking here, of course, of the religious dimension that invites in the disowning to place our disarray and disorder into the hands of God, who exercises formidable power with regard to our failures. Many religious traditions symbolize the owning and disowning, the denial and assertion aspects of forgiveness, with rituals whereby people confess their sins and are absolved of them. In that act of absolution, past sins are put behind us once and for all because God has the power to remove and to forget, as if these events never happened in terms of the way He relates to us.

There are many in Protestant traditions which have long dissociated themselves from this practice who commend confessing to one's brothers and sisters as theologically and psychologically sound. "Protestants talked a great deal about the forgiveness of God," John Claypool once preached, "but we forgot how *to do* confession and repentance and the receiving of forgiveness. As a result, for many now in the Free Church tradition, we do not know how to get rid of our sins. We continue to carry around the whole load of the past without any relief."[16]

Central to the teaching of the early church was the injunction to "confess your sins to one another" (James 5:16). Some consider this practice worth recovering because of the level of self-awareness that is raised. "The primary purpose of confession is to keep people aware of their true condition," wrote Charles Hanna, "of the tension between the good and evil in themselves."[17] Dietrich Bonhoeffer considered the practice of confessing valuable because "a man who confesses his sins in the presence of a brother knows that he is no longer alone with himself; he experiences the presence of God in the reality of the other person."[18]

The Roman Catholic tradition, which has preserved auricular confession throughout the centuries, has recently revised and refreshed its rite of reconciliation.[19] Among Roman Catholics it was generally recognized that the former rite never had an easy time aligning itself with the theology of penance. When the theology of penance revealed the intimate love of God, the rite often reflected an impersonal, mechanical, and routine procedure. When the theology called for a ritual to express reunion with a community, the rite reflected isolation and alienation from a social understanding of sin and conversion. When the theology needed a sign to communicate healing, the ritual, for some, resembled a criminal court where a judge acquitted or condemned, but never forgave or loved. In its most anemic state, the closeted secrecy and anonymity of the old rite sometimes fostered an unhealthy self-deprecation and a morbid dwelling on sin that was on a collision course with the theology of penance which announced wholeness and rebirth.

Such an analysis, of course, indicts the old rite at its

weakest and most vulnerable points. There were, certainly, significant transformations through ownings and disownings in the former practice of confession. The new rite simply intends to let those encounters be more accessible and less obscure than before. It tries to make the signs more transparent to the reality expressed, and in the process, the new rite harmonizes the ritual with the very substantive theology of penance.

One of the more obvious changes in the new rite is its vocabulary. No longer is this sacrament referred to as "confession," and that is just as well, because "going to confession" sounded as if the penitent was the focus of the event and that absolution was granted as a reward for submitting oneself to the humbling experience of telling one's sins.

There is a concern in the new rite for unearthing the roots of our sinfulness that we are often blind to. Notre Dame University theologian James Burtchaell once wrote that penitents must ask the ministers of this sacrament "to help them discover what never gets on their consciences."[20] He had in mind those furtive but significant sins that too often go unnoticed, and because they go unnoticed, they go unrepented and unforgiven.

The conversion at the heart of the experience of confession is about these more pervasive and perverse orientations, and less about perfunctory shopping lists of sins routinely confessed and routinely, if validly, absolved. Conversion is about death and life, and this is the sensitivity of the new rite. It is not a scrupulous search for minutiae, but a sincere desire to discover the patterns of evil in our hearts that disable us from doing the good we would do, but do not.

The new rite shifts the emphasis from what the penitent is doing, to what God is doing, and what God is doing is reconciling us to Himself. To reconcile means to bring together that which belongs together but which is apart. To reconcile means to bind, to heal, to effect wholeness, to bring peace. The act of reconciliation brings together God and humankind; it brings together men and women as they are and men and women as they ought to be. Reconciliation is a hard vocation that ultimately cost Jesus His life. And any participation in this sacrament will enable a sharing in the victory of that event.

This sacrament, of course, was never intended to reaffirm the status quo, to encourage routine and catalogue-style confessions, or to reinforce feelings of self-disesteem or self-hatred. The power, rather, lies in the affirmation that because God is working, change is possible and the promise of healing is real. The new rite credits this power as a gift of the Holy Spirit, and so it may be. Traditionally the theological role of the Spirit has been to teach Jesus and all Christians their identity as sons and daughters of God. In uncovering that identity, it is the Spirit who filters light on our disorder and displacement so that we can know our sins, who gives us strength to acknowledge them simply, and who remains as comforter through the ego-death that penance and its encounter with truth requires. The result is similar to all brushes with truth: an exhilarating freedom and a purifying release from bonds that held us back.

When all is said and done, confession is a song of gratitude because we are able to claim the presence and power of God in our lives. We have been confronted. We have been converted, turned around. In the end we have gone through a process where we sense the truth about ourselves and discover that even then we are loved beyond our imaginings. "We do not confess our faults in order that God may become better acquainted with them, but in order that the concreteness of words will increase our own understanding."[21]

That self-understanding is transferable to our brothers and sisters who are in need of forgiveness, and it sensitizes us to remain compassionate to them. "Forgiveness is only real," suggests Henri Nouwen, for the compassionate person "who has discovered the weakness of his friends and the sins of his enemy in his own heart and is willing to call every human being his brother."[22]

While the forgiving part of us looks forward to the completeness of the act of forgiveness—toward someone accepting our gift—this is not the same as our placing conditions on forgiveness. Our forgiveness has to be unconditional, with no strings attached, or it isn't forgiveness. I can't exact acts of self-abasement from someone, I can't demand humiliating gestures and public apologies. I can't catalogue demands. Forgiveness is best done quietly with no witnesses, and it may be best received that way, too. "Keep your deeds of mercy secret, and your Father who sees in secret will repay you" (Matt. 6:4).

What does the forgiver do when the gift of forgiveness is not received? When the gift is laughed at or rejected?

What does the person in need of forgiveness do when no one is offering the gift? What does that person do when an apology is not received, and instead of a handshake, a snarl is offered instead?

Both wait. Both are called on to be watchful, to be vigilant, to wait for the right moment to extend forgiveness or to receive it. Love is patient, and we learn the truth of this lesson most especially in this very ennobled form of love and giving that forgiveness is.

Forgiveness Is a Power

A power is a directing force in my life, an energizing influence. I can talk of people who exert power over me if I want to convey to you a sense of their importance in my life as they influence my thinking and my actions. That power, of course, can be for good or for ill, depending on how congruent the actions are with my freedom.

When I am hurt, physically or spiritually, my wounds have power over me, they tell me what I can or can't do. And when I am wounded spiritually by my own failure or someone else's failure in the many guises these can take, I am likewise led by the power of those memories and those experiences.

Forgiveness is a power that counteracts, that serves as an antidote to the energy of the pain that directs me. Forgiveness is a power that says that as deep as the pain may be, there is a strength and a comfort that goes beneath the pain so that I am finally led not by the wound but by a force more commanding than the hurt.

A great degree of consciousness is required here. We are not asked to bypass our grief or to count it as inconsequential. We are asked to confront it, to discern its origin, to feel it, and then to forgive with all our wits about us. That kind of conscious, deliberate confrontation lets me go to the very bottom of my hurt and, metaphorically, cleans out the wound and cauterizes it. Only then can healing begin.

Let a six-inch ruler standing upright represent the range of pains that we have borne in our lifetime. Slight offenses measure in the one- to two-inch sections, while significant losses and hurts measure more.

If I have been profoundly hurt and my resentment is throbbing at the very bottom of this measure, I have only three alternatives:

1. I can put a bandage on top of the wound, pretending that it is not serious and that it doesn't require any further attention. But wounds inflicted psychically and spiritually bear comparison to physical ones, and the process of their cures is similar. Splintered fingers that are not cleaned will not heal properly. In fact, if they're not taken care of at all, they can disfigure, they can fester, they can even infect the total organism. And a cut that is treated with a bandage when it requires more thorough medical attention may cause recurrent pain and take longer to heal, if in fact it heals at all.

2. I can be led by the pain or hurt. My interests, my actions, my choices will then be made in light of the pain. And if you, as my friend, touch that pain—accidentally or deliberately—you set off a reflex action in me that allows me to relive the original painful experience and to be led by it once again.

3. Or I can allow forgiveness to inch its way down to the level of my pain. Forgiveness can extend even beyond the hurts that have been directing me so that eventually forgiveness commands.

A young man rejected in a relationship forgives his former girlfriend and no longer is led by that pain.

A middle-aged man, depressed by feelings of inadequacy, forgives his father's relentless pushing him toward excelling, and is able to be led by forgiving love rather than resentment.

A wife is able to forgive herself her unreasonable perfectionism and can live an unshackled future.

These transfers of power are occasions to rejoice because they mark the end of a fierce and enervating struggle and inaugurate the blessed peace of healing.

There's another way to look at forgiveness as a power and that is when we acknowledge that forgiveness is not just an idea, but an event. Forgiveness is not just words, but deeds. When we forgive or when we are forgiven, something radical happens.

There is an image in the Old Testament that suggests, paradigmatically, what happens when any of us extends forgiveness. The image from Psalm 103 is that Yahweh has the power to separate us from our sins as far as the East is from the West.

For a minute, let's consider that image. The offender and the offense are bound together; to many people, like the Pharisees, the offender is identical with the offense. Then forgiveness is extended and accepted, and at that point the offender is separated from the offense as far as is imaginable.

How far might that be?

Well, it seems more than fortuitous—and, I believe, inspired—that the distance is measured not by northness and southness but by eastness and westness. North and south have two precise poles, geographically measurable, so that we are able to head to the North Pole, but at one point we stop going north and begin to go south. Likewise, we can head toward the South Pole, but at one point in our journey we will stop heading south and begin to head north. There are limits to northness and southness. But if we travel east, we will go on indefinitely because there is no East Pole; there is no limit to eastness. If we traveled west, we would travel on forever and ever without changing direction.

Thus, if we were going to reach for a term descriptive of the total way that Yahweh forgives (and *we* are expected to), it would be by telling the person in need of forgiveness that this act of forgiveness is so powerful that as far as the East is from the West, so, too, shall your sins be removed from you. Removed. Not lessened, not weakened, not pushed away a mite, but removed—so that you will no longer be defined by that offense, so that the offense will no longer direct our relationship—removed as far as we can possibly imagine. That far are we separated from our offenses. This is how God handles sin, and only the most radical term approaches being descriptive about it.

When God forgives, something decisive happens. When we forgive, something decisive happens, too. That decisive something has enormous impact on relationships. Matthew and Dennis Linn describe the results of one such occasion in an inner-healing workshop, where men and women, once divorced and now remarried, hoped for a healing of hostilities that they felt toward their former spouses.[23] These retreatants were led through a healing process over the course of a weekend, slowly and meditatively, even to the point of prayerfully uncovering ways in which they felt they could grow from the painful experiences and separations of their first marriages.

After a year the group gathered again and talked about the differences the healing workshop made in their lives. The Linns report that "out of the seven who forgave a former spouse after years of resentment, five found that their former spouses had suddenly made an effort to forgive and build a bridge toward them. One suddenly called a week after the workshop, and another traveled two thousand miles to see his family, and another wrote his first letter in ten silent years."[24]

The Linn brothers, following the perceptive counsel of Agnes Sanford, encourage their retreat and workshop participants to forgive and then to return home and expect to see a change in relationships with the person forgiven.

Forgiveness, then, exerts the most formidable power of all when it enables change. Forgiveness changes circumstances every bit as tangibly as sin does. An act of pardon is just as real an event as an act of sin. And when I admit my sinfulness and acknowledge my unloving actions, I can actually change. I can alter reality!

Karl Menninger comes at this truth from a slightly different angle. Founder of the Menninger Clinic and author of *Whatever Became of Sin?* Dr. Menninger tells us that a sinner is one who is responsible for his or her unloving actions and *can change*. If one cannot reform, then the structure of a prison or penal institution is the answer. If one is ill and is not responsible for the harm he or she is doing, then a mental hospital is the alternative. The sinner is different from these cases: he or she acknowledges sin and takes responsibility for change—a change ultimately effected through the grace of God.

Forgiveness is an event, not an idea, and it comes full circle at the moment I discover myself and claim myself as sinner. At that moment, we receive divine forgiveness as "that 'making right' of our lives which occurs when we turn away from fighting ourselves, and others, and the truth itself, and turn trustfully toward the divine power which surrounds us and can work through us."[25] Through this extraordinary experience of reconciliation, our past failures and unsolved current problems notwithstanding, we are actually made "more lovable, more discerning, more capable of devoting (ourselves) to goods which enrich humanity."[26]

CHAPTER V

What Enables Forgiveness

PROBABLY one of the most accurate analogies to use in thinking about the forgiveness process is its similarity to the process of healing physical pain.

Like accident victims, people who need to forgive are injured, hurting, bleeding. They have been deeply and harmfully affected by some person or some event—or both—and they experience the residue of this kind of experience: shock, temporary paralysis, depression, and sometimes external, sometimes internal wounds, or sometimes both. Time, tests, and X rays frequently reveal the extent of injuries not immediately apparent, or at least not apparent to the naked eye.

What we find when we take a look at the medical procedure is that a priority of the medical world is to relieve pain. Even before a patient is put onto an emergency-room examination table, it's likely that the bleeding has been cleaned away and an anesthetic administered. The cleansing and the anesthetic don't deny the pain— they don't pretend that the pain isn't there or that the wounds aren't in need of attention. The cleansing provides a view of the extent of the injuries, and the anesthetic enables some kind of distance from the wound for the patient, and for those ministering to the patient, to take stock of the situation and, in tandem, to plan the shortest route to recovery.

When it comes to forgiveness, we could learn something helpful from this procedure. The immediate goal in our physical as well as inner healings is the same: to relieve pain before we can talk about strategies for forgiving.

Medically as well as spiritually, there are many ways that pain can be relieved; to discuss three possibilities hardly exhausts the subject.

Relieving Pain

BY DISTANCE   Sometimes pain is relieved by distancing two people from each other.

I know of a competitive pressure that severely agonized a nine-year-old twin son whose parents sensed the tension and wanted to facilitate a reconciliation between brothers.

Since the boys were in continuous contact with each other twenty-four hours a day, the parents saw value in separating them from each other for several hours each day—preferably during their school hours when the competition was in full force.

There were several options open to the parents. In the process of thinking about distancing them from each other geographically, they considered sending one boy to a boarding school and letting the other remain in the local private school. Another alternative was to send the two boys to different boarding schools. Still a third alternative was to send each one to a separate local school, a decision that would keep the family together (a highly desirable state during the working out of the forgiveness), while also abating the tension between the two brothers sufficiently to allow civility to reign before reconciliation could claim a grip on the situation.

They chose the third alternative, and as it turned out, this strategy was very helpful to the brothers and the parents. A great deal of the tension was deflected and the hours the boys spent together at home were less harried and more harmonious from the beginning of the experiment. Both parents were happy that they didn't choose one of the more drastic alternatives. To have separated the boys by sending one away to boarding school may also have eased the problem, but it would have done so at the expense of separating the family, and it may never have given them a chance to work things through together as a loving unit committed to one another.

On the other hand, there is the situation of an alcoholic friend of mine whose condition deteriorated severely over the summer. By October the seven- and nine-year-old daughters could expect their alcoholic mother to unleash a violent temper almost every day when they returned from school.

The scene that faced the husband-father in the evening was chaotic and tragic: the girls cowering, and on occasion now, being physically abused. When the holidays rolled around, everyone lived through a most pathetic Christmas. The husband, at the end of his rope with his wife's irrational, ego-centered behavior, was barely able to cope with this latest hurt. The children, inured to the behavior pattern but too young to analyze and interpret it, were devastated.

Taking stock of the situation (the need of the girls to have a mother, her inability to function as a mother at that time, and her need for a supportive context that neither the husband—because of his job—nor the girls—because of their age—were able to provide), the parents decided, in careful consultation with the girls, on a course of action that allowed the mother to spend weekdays at a sanitarium in Connecticut, seventy-five miles from their house, and weekends at home with the family.

After the first month of this experiment the mother's spirits began to lift. Her improvement since then brought along new career interests that she will probably pursue in months ahead. The family agrees that the weekdays go by very swiftly and that the weekends are fun, and yet serious times, that tension has been reduced significantly, and that genuine forgiveness has begun and many hurts have already healed.

There is no one rule about distancing and relieving pain. A good rule of thumb is to choose the least drastic alternative and then pray that a wise person will help us to know what that might be.

BY A THERAPEUTIC RELATIONSHIP Similarly, when we are close to a couple living through struggling times within a marriage, when each person is experiencing unrelenting, unabated hostility and a compounding of fractures and concussions (metaphorically speaking), a relief of the pain is often desperately called for.

That relief does not have to necessitate one person moving to Phoenix while the other remains in Boston; nor does relief mean a term of separation—a month, a year—

although each of these may be what certain situations call for. Once again, let's advocate the least drastic, but often no less effective remedy.

In the case of marital problems, a therapeutic relationship frequently relieves the pain. For him, for her, there is then a place where disappointments can be aired, where fury can be vented, where frustration can be spoken openly. It is enormously relieving within a marriage, or within any stress-filled relationship between two (or more) people, for each of the persons feeling the stress and pain to have a therapeutic (healing) relationship. Then, when the persons live through each other's weaknesses and failures, they know that, even as they live through these feelings, there is a place they can go where they can soon discuss the situation with some objectivity, sensitivity, wisdom, and assistance. In that way at least the wounds, though deep, can be kept clean, withdrawal and total warfare—direct opposites—will not be the only alternatives, and in the process of the cleaning, no infections will begin.

The goal, remember, is not simply to relieve the pain. It is to relieve the pain so that a healing can take place. That's why, all too frequently, a friend doesn't quite fill the bill. We're not looking for a shoulder to lean on; we're looking for someone who can help us see the situation as it is, interpret it for us, and encourage us in our attempts to work things out.

If we have friends like this, we are fortunate indeed. Frequently enough friends and family, anxious for us (and *themselves*) to avoid pain, encourage us through righteous platitudes about the correctness of our throwing in the towel, and they anesthetize us to the work at hand, which is the very tough business of forgiveness.

The question we have to ask ourselves when we turn to distancing as the way to ease pain is, "Is this strategy going to facilitate the healing that forgiveness is?" or "Is it going to numb me to it, and in the long run have me avoid forgiveness?"

BY CONFRONTATION A friend of mine, an executive with a large bank in New York City, is currently working through a series of setbacks and hurts on his job. As best he can assess the situation, the occasion for a chain of humiliations has been the boss's nephew, who has been eyeing my friend's job for the last half-year. An assortment of unkind manipulative gymnastics has made life at the office miserable for my friend and, more importantly, has practically severed a twenty-year friendship my friend has had with his boss. The resulting sense of betrayal has brought along with it strong feelings of hostility and resentment toward my friend's employer.

There are several ways that the pain in this situation could be dealt with, and in the last six months my friend has considered:

(1) Submitting a resignation:
At least this gesture would ease the pain of humiliation that this man experiences in the presence of his co-workers. And it would appear to everyone that he is in the driver's seat, commanding the moves—the doer and not the receiver of action.

(2) Undermining support for his boss:
This strategy has little to commend it, except for the cathartic effect of retaliation: to want to hurt the person hurting us. But that effect is short-lived and its aftermath brings even more guilt into the picture. In the long run, that guilt of implicating others further exacerbates the pain.

82

(3) Entering a counseling relationship:
This has its possibilities.

(4) Confronting his boss with his pain:
For my friend, this has the obvious disadvantage of exposing him as vulnerable, of possibly making him experience rebuff and thus more pain—but in the end, it's what he chose to do. He saw two advantages to this approach. First, it rested with some sense of security (precarious, to be sure), on the strength of a twenty-year relationship. It honored that relationship even though it was then going through some rocky times. Secondly, it might be the source of new and helpful information about the situation. While emotions were escalating and feelings were being hurt—on both sides—data were being processed through third and fourth persons. Now, at least, there would be a chance to share facts. This, in a spirit of friendship, and provided tempers stayed cooled, might be beneficial in assessing the situation and considering alternatives.

Which is exactly what happened.

Instead of falling on the defensive, the employer frankly admitted to the employee the bind he was in.

"I don't know what to do," he told my friend. "I'm pressured by my wife who wants me to find a secure place for her nephew in the firm, and my nephew has fixed on your job. Your loyalty to the firm and your friendship pulls me the other way and I don't know how else to resolve this."

Fortunately, my friend had some ideas.

Fortunately, my friend was also able to consider the possibility of forgiveness. Otherwise, to save face, he may have had to grandstand some gesture of outrage or superiority that wouldn't have allowed a working out of the problems in his career *or* friendship. My friend recognized a weakness in his employer and was unwilling to consider it the last or most significant word about him.

The episode taught this friend of mine the danger of living with untested assumptions. Had he not confronted his employer he never would have known why he was asked to leave. Learning the reasons behind someone's offensive and even cruel behavior toward us doesn't change the fact of the behavior—it still happened—but it does give us information that can be helpful to us in dealing with our hurts. To appreciate the stresses and tensions of others is to help us strategize for forgiveness, to make that idea an event in our lives.

It is now six months since this event first began. It touched many more than the lives of a nephew, a boss, and an employee. It was capable of destroying many more than three lives. The effort at understanding and forgiving yielded great dividends for all.

Strategizing for Forgiveness

EXPANDING THE CONTEXT OF THE SITUATION We are prepared, when the pain has been soothed, to strategize for forgiveness. We are prepared for the best part.

The best part is tackling the situation now—with whatever reserves of strength we've stored up, with our support systems—and learning to forgive. In that learning there is the promise of peace that surpasses any human understanding, there is the promise of growth, of becoming the person we know we are.

There is, of course, also a temptation at this juncture.

Once we "feel better" we can be seduced into believing that feeling better is enough. Andras Angyal, a good guide in these areas, tells us that, frequently enough, people enter the psychotherapeutic relationship not to be better, but simply to feel better.[1]

So, we can settle here in this state of feeling better. We can learn a strategy or two about how to return to this feeling whenever we are hurt. We can learn to cope. People do it in marriages, in parent-child relationships, and in friendships.

Or we can learn to bypass forgiveness. In our moment of euphoria, of feeling better, we can skim over the hurt, decline facing it again, and move on to other things. Living under this anesthetic for a whole lifetime has got to be a less-than-desirable way to spend one's life. But it's a way people frequently choose.

We have already discussed the limitations of living without forgiveness or living by bypassing forgiveness. We simply want to indicate here that these are obvious options.

If non-forgiveness is self-destructive, and bypassing forgiveness is ultimately nonproductive, then we want to move on to the creative activity that is forgiveness itself. We are helped mostly, in this process of forgiveness, by *enlarging the context of the situation that surrounds our hurt.*

It becomes enormously important that we be able to see the one who is hurting us as a person, and not only the cause of our pain. This is what enlarging the context of the situation means. When we widen that context, we are able to see the offender as a person, with limitations, inadequacies, flaws, imperfections, unhealed hurts—all of which contribute to that person's inability to love. When that kind of framework is established, part of my response becomes to set that person free to love. I feel part anger, part resentment, part hurt, and also part setting that person free to love. The last is a growing, emerging part that eventually enables me to forgive.

Several years ago, when I moved with my family to a different city, my seven-year-old son started the school year with a head-on conflict with the twelve-year-old school bully. On the first day of school the bully pushed my son off the school bus, ordered him to carry his books home, and made the prospect of going to school a horror for him.

As a mother, my first reaction was a siege of anger at someone larger and older taking advantage of someone less powerful. That emotion ruled my thoughts and helped me frame some strategies, several of which came to mind in rapid-fire succession. The way I saw things, I had several options. My first option was to "fight fire with fire." I could confront the twelve-year-old bully with the authority and strength of my adulthood and tell him he'd have to deal with me if there was a repeat performance. (I didn't think my son would suffer because of parental interference.) My second option was to visit with the bully's eighth-grade teacher or the principal, both of whom I had come to know during the summer months prior to the opening of school. I could, I was sure, enlist their disciplinary support. Third, I could approach the boy's parents. They were across-the-street neighbors, and I had noticed that, unexpectedly or predictably—I'm never sure which in these situations—they were strict disciplinarians and would see to it that remedial action was taken. I can honestly tell you that all of these options occurred to me in less than a minute—all of the strategies I needed to handle the situation.

I was on my way to implementing the one I would judge to be the best of the solutions, when my son reminded me, "But if he stops picking on me, he'll only start picking on someone else. Some other kid in the school is going to get it if it's not me!"

Soon after, my son appraised the situation by saying, "I'd rather find some way of getting along with him because I'll probably be living with him for a long time."

Both of these observations made me realize how obviously my strategies were schemes to retaliate, to cut this twelve-year-old child out of our lives, to cancel any possibility of a relationship with him. One thing for sure, my strategies weren't moving in the direction of establishing peace, of being responsible in some way for this other child, of building bridges.

It took time—days, as I remember—before I could look at the situation differently. When I did, my emotions were still with my child, my son. With him, as well, were my instincts to protect, to guard, to keep him free from injury. What also emerged from someplace in me—and this was greatly aided by my son Christopher's comments—was a feeling of responsibility for our neighbor. I realized that if I removed Christopher from the fray another child would be victimized, so I would be solving only part of the problem and transferring another part to someone else. That analysis helped me to look for a way to confront the situation with an eye to enabling our neighbors' child to be "free" enough not to be a bully.

My goal shifted. The goal was no longer wanting to get even, to "fight fire with fire," as I had wanted to do in the beginning. My goal—my family's goal—was to set this child free to love more than he was apparently capable of doing at the time.

Once the goal was established, my interest lay in finding the strategy to reach that goal. What surprised me was that several of the strategies I had thought of before were strategies that I thought of again. This time, however, they were strategies in light of another goal and they were not goals in themselves.

What that means is that this new goal, to set our little neighbor free to love, could probably be reached with the help of my original goals—to confront him or work through his teachers or his parents. Whatever the strategy, though, it would have to be selected with the overriding goal in mind. There is a difference between soliciting the assistance of a principal, dumping the problem in her lap, and thereby severing a relationship with the bully, and the other choice of enlisting her support to strengthen the relationship on other grounds of compatibility and support. I selected the latter.

I approached the principal and told her that we wanted to work through the problem for our good, for the benefit of the other child who was harassing mine, and for any children who might be affected in the future. The principal was cooperative. She and I saw the need the bully had for attention, and we set on a course to affirm him, enlist his support with the smaller children, and encourage him as an older boy to be helpful to my son. It didn't work. We tried again. And again.

We found there was no magical formula. We found that love, above all, is patient. And we found that love, in the end—in the end that looks as though it will never come—in that end, love triumphs.

I have told this story in various places to different people. I am enormously conscious of the "smallness" of the story. It isn't working through the bigger issues of forgiving the betrayal of a loved one; it doesn't work through forgiving wounds that cut more deeply and for more prolonged periods than mine. And I have become very aware that the point of the story for me is not whether talking the thing over with the principal was the best way to handle the situation. The point was for me not to do anything unless I was motivated by love of this other child.

Other people have suggested what seem to me to be far better and more sensitive solutions. One dear, loving woman approached me one evening after a lecture I gave and suggested, "Did you ever think of just letting the children work it out themselves? I've often regretted making my children's lives more complicated by interfering into what they seem to be able to handle perfectly well on their own!" Frankly, it never occurred to me, but since then I have thought about the merits of it and other ideas. It seems to me that any number of them could have been effective if their intention "served" the goal to set someone free to love. Conversely, any number of them could have failed if they were used to play a game of one-upmanship, to get even, to crush a child's spirit, to punish.

I've reflected, too, that in spite of the "petiteness" of the situation, I found it grueling and very difficult to work through. My emotions were almost continually in tension. On one side there were feelings of tenderness and affection toward my little neighbor. I tried to think of him as a mother would: a dear and precious child in need of loving correction and discipline. On the other side were feelings of anger, rage, and frustration. In my mind I punched him in the nose dozens of times. And in the middle of these two sets of emotions was conflict—I was torn in two directions—which resolved itself, with the sustained help of prayer, in favor of forgiving. I lived to see my son and this other child on friendly terms. There were days when I believed that if this would happen, it would happen in another world, or long after I passed through this one. There were days I thought it wasn't worth the effort. And there were days—and these were the most joyous—when I felt we were part of unlocking a love that became twisted and gnarled and wasn't able to function.

Lastly, I've reflected many times on how different things would be in my life, and in the lives of families, communities, and countries, if we all worked with this goal in mind. Maybe we'd all be too exhausted to fight, because loving is enormously exhausting. But for whatever reason, we'd surely have a different world.

I recently met the assistant principal of a private school in New Brunswick, New Jersey. The school had no principal, or rather, the principal, I was advised, was the Lord. The philosophy of the school, the assistant principal explained, was summed up in the fifth chapter of Paul's second letter to the Corinthians: "Just love." In practice, what this meant was that the school accepted the fact that there was no problem they could not lovingly handle within their walls, and no child who was not welcome. Brain-damaged, retarded, and brilliant students were all part of the mix. And to top it all off, no child had to fear expulsion. The assistant principal rattled off a list of the administration's dealings with vandalism, violence, and incorrigibility, and demonstrated their presence as a forgiving community in the midst of problems endemic to inner city, racially balanced schools.

I can tell you that the atmosphere at that school on a rainy November day was so warm and lovely that it would have disarmed its most virulent critic. Had I seen all of this on an island nestled somewhere in the remote waters of the Pacific, I would have suspected it was the climate, or the water the people drank, that enabled such civility, such genuine concern, such obvious cooperation, and such helpful, forgiving, tender, and appreciative attitudes toward one another. But this was a situation in my own backyard, different from any school I had ever seen before. And far from denying awareness of how it came to be that way, the strategy was announced to anyone who wanted to listen: Just the Gospel in action. This is what it looks like when people forgive each other.

If there is anything I'd like to underscore in this discussion about strategies for forgiveness, it's only this: there is no *one* way.

There are those I know who propose turning the other cheek as the answer in all situations, but I have watched situations where turning the other cheek has only exacerbated the hostility and made forgiveness an even more remote possibility. There are times when turning the other cheek is viewed not as a gesture of love, but as a sign of arrogance and pomposity, and in those situations it does more harm than good.

Even the New Testament tells of different ways to strategize for forgiveness. Sometimes we are encouraged to turn the other cheek (Matt. 5:39), sometimes to confront those who have wronged us (Matt. 8:15–18), sometimes to admonish (1 Cor. 4:14). It all depends on the situation and the people involved.

The point is that there is no surefire answer that applies across the board. But there is one motivation that applies at all times, in every single instance, without qualification, and that is the goal to set someone free, which overrides and counsels any and all of our strategies. Once that vision is perceived, then we have been able to enlarge the context, and we have taken the most important step toward forgiveness.

That goal, of course, is applicable to both big and small events in need of reconciliation. More often than not, however, it works itself out in the mundane, daily struggles we face—those continual trespassings that need "forgiving, dismissing, in order to make it possible for life to go on by constantly releasing men from what they have done unknowingly."[2] These small-scale victories are of enormous importance—if the ripple-effect theory holds true—for many more than a small range of relationships.

One of the common daily situations is a domestic one and involves the relationship between fathers and their grown sons, and between mothers and their grown daughters. In one such instance, a middle-aged woman with children in high school and college, a career of her own, and a husband long rooted in his profession, was living out a good marriage within a happy home. Objectively the setting exudes confidence and generativity, yet the persistent *bête noire* in the life of this woman was her mother, who visited twice yearly and left this daughter, after each of those visits, upset, tired, bored, frustrated, angry, and feeling like a failure. The average recovery period after a visit was three months.

For the mother, good was never good enough, and this was the source of the conflict.

"This dinner would have been marvelous if you didn't overcook the meat."

"This room would be lovely if it had fewer chairs."

"Do you always overdose your plants with so much water?"

We know that no one's feelings are caused by others, that our feelings are caused by our own emotional responses, our own choices and reactions. That, of course, is the subject of another book, or of other books already written that amplify this important subject for us.[3]

What is pertinent for us here is that once our emotions are recognized, our successful wife-mother-career woman has two basic options confronting her when her mother announces one of her dreaded visits. First, she can anticipate that her mother will hurt her again, will chip away at her self-image, will denigrate her accomplishments, and will leave her in a state of paralysis—that is, she can look at her mother's visit as an evil to be endured. That anticipation, incidentally, has the aura of a self-fulfilling prophecy about it.

Second, she can pull her own feelings together and take a look at her mother, not as a villain, but as someone who does the things she does, and says the things she says, because she is not totally free to do otherwise. She's probably doing the best she can under the limitations and circumstances of her own life. Instead of being generous, the mother feels compelled to criticize; instead of giving, she is resistant; instead of being vulnerable, she is combative.

The perspective then is not "How will I scoop myself up after she leaves?", but "What can I do before she comes, while she's here, or after she leaves, to set her free to love so that she doesn't have to behave this way anymore?"

A particularly effervescent woman I know planned to shift her strategies in light of the goal of enlarging the context of a mother-in-law's visit, and found herself giggling in good humor at her visitor's many imperious commands and suggestions. "Once I realized," she told me, "that her own life was filled with unhealed hurts that were never dealt with and that, in turn, never allowed her to relax and praise others, I couldn't be devastated by her criticisms. There used to be times after these visits when I threatened my husband that I would leave him forever if he insisted that she could visit us again. Now, I was able to deal, at least partially, with the dissonant chords she struck."

Does this sound condescending? Admittedly, the line here is thin between condescension and love. When I condescend, however, I stoop from my pedestal to your benighted position. When I love, I never lose sight of the fact that even in your fumbling gestures you are loving me. The condescender sees the act as an affront and tries to rise above it. The forgiver sees the offensive act as camouflaged—but genuine—love.

For the mother-in-law, the good natured chuckling defused the time bomb, lessened the tension. "I don't think you're taking me seriously," she said to her daughter-in-law, quizzically.

"So many times," confided the daughter-in-law, "I had speeches prepared, answers to situations rehearsed. And this time, with caring, I was able to say, spontaneously and sincerely, 'I don't take *this part* of you seriously, that's true, but I take *you* very seriously.'" That simple comment jolted the relationship out of its deadlock.

All situations don't end as fortuitously.

Sometimes it becomes necessary to suggest that a visit not take place. Sometimes a confrontation is in order. Whatever route is chosen, the results in the long run are most heartening when they come from a desire to set someone free to love. When strategies are employed to prove someone wrong or to get even, no matter what the immediate result, we will be left unsatisfied in the long run.

A frequently used medium to settle disputes, if not to effect forgiveness, is the law. There are those who tell me that once the legal process is invoked, forgiveness will never take place. And there are those who maintain that recourse to the legal process is absolutely necessary against persons whose behavior is offensive and hurtful, as a strategy to shake them and wake them up to the issues and responsibilities at stake.

Once again, what strategy we employ isn't as important as why we choose it. If I pursue a lawsuit to eke out revenge, to harass, to embarrass, to confuse the issues, to humiliate, then I obviously have as my motive something other than setting someone free to love.

But if I have importuned you, and if the family or community has gone its mile with you in trying to live with you outside the strictures of the legal process, we may have to choose to invoke it. How careful we have to be here of our motives, of what we hear in the interchange between us and the one who is hurting us!

The New Testament reference in Matthew 18:15–17 is helpful.

> If your brother should commit some wrong against you, go and point out his fault, but keep it between the two of you. If he listens to you, you have won your brother over. If he does not listen, summon another, so that every case may stand on the word of two or three witnesses. If he ignores them, refer it to the church. If he ignores even the church, then treat him as would a Gentile or a tax collector.

Contextually, the aim of the eighteenth chapter of the Gospel of Matthew is forgiveness. In some cases, it would seem, severe disciplinary measures may have to be taken.

We begin by confronting our offender in private to avoid embarrassment. It is our hope that that will suffice and peace will be established. If that fails, we move to a semilegal procedure wherein we involve witnesses to determine the offender's obstinacy, as well as, perhaps, our own reading of the situation. A witness, then, can also help us keep our own motives pure by noticing whether we are overreacting and perhaps misjudging reactions. When even that fails as a strategy, we ask the community at large to concur in our decision to treat that person as one worthy of respect, love, and concern, but also as one who is no longer part of the inner circle of the family.

The offender is never out of relationship with the community, and though we have to look somewhere other than Matthew to see how this bonding is continued, we might fairly surmise that the second letter to the Corinthians, Chapter 2, explains what was paradigmatic for all early Christians:

"[When] the punishment already inflicted by the majority on such a one is enough, you should now relent and support him so that he may not be crushed by too great a weight of sorrow. I therefore beg you to reaffirm your love for him" (2 Cor. 2:6–7).

This confrontational, disciplinary strategy, then, rests on the premise that the offender has to accept the invitation to own and to disown his "sins," "offenses," or "wrongdoings," in order to be able to accept forgiveness. And, sometimes, the offender needs help in being made aware of his or her culpability.

Once again, in *some* situations, this may be the appropriate strategy, and must not be regarded as callous and retributive. "To be 'convicted of sin,'" writes Seward Hiltner, "is ultimately good rather than bad news. . . . But the road to conviction of sin is through understanding and love, not through denunciation."[4]

The caution cited in 2 Corinthians undergirds this strategy with the compassion, understanding, and love required. It tempers justice with mercy and leaves the scissors lying on the table, unused. This has the capability of being a strategy of service and freedom, and it only makes sense when perceived from that angle.

I know of an instance, not personal to me, where the lessons of Matthew 18 and 2 Corinthians 5 were tested and led to an undesired but necessary legal process.

Having closed their summer home for the season, the father of a family of three young boys headed back from Cape Cod to New York City on a rainy September night. Suddenly, the station wagon he was driving was struck head-on by a pickup truck being driven on the wrong side of the road. The driver of the station wagon suffered injuries so severe that he wound up spending over eighteen months in a hospital, and his vision in one eye was permanently impaired. The driver of the truck was uninjured.

Early in her husband's convalescence, the wife of the victim was importuned by the driver of the truck not to press criminal charges against him. A twenty-eight-year-old Vietnam veteran, he had a wife and two little daughters of his own to care for and was struggling to get his feet on the ground. The job he was on call for, and close to being hired for, ironically, was that of school-bus driver with seniority, which meant if all things panned out, he would have his first permanent job in four years. Moved by the story, the wife of the victim relayed the story to her husband, and both of them, surrounded by continual reminders of the accident in his hospital room, decided to forgo the legal suit.

Several days after the decision was made, the wife of the man responsible for the accident came to the hospital; she felt in conscience responsible to make some facts known. Several times a week, after bouts of heavy drinking that seemed to occasion an acute depression, her husband would head off in their pickup truck (that and a used trailer, both uninsured, were their only possessions) and would career across fields and backroads alike, set on frightening the wits out of passengers in other cars. His favorite sport was riding on the wrong side of the road, forcing any driver who happened to come along to veer off into the trees or embankments. Twice she accompanied him on these potentially lethal roller-coaster trips, and was convinced he was in need of professional psychiatric help, which she felt he would never seek voluntarily. Poor as they were, her greatest anxiety was that he would, in fact, get the job as a school-bus driver. Since this was the first reported accident (the others, it seemed, happened too fast for others to know what was happening and to determine their cause), she hoped it would force the issues into the open.

The new evidence brought about a revised decision. From his hospital bed, the victim and his wife explained to the man responsible for the accident that they still remained forgiving, but that in light of new information, they knew the gravity of the implications of their silence for the school-bus job.

Pressing charges meant an automatic license suspension for six months and a compulsory rehabilitation program for reinstatement. The victim knew if he did not pursue this course of action that there was no likelihood of any change in this destructive behavior. The couple promised help in finding a counselor, if that was wanted, and action, not just words, in finding another job.

The couple in that hospital room—husband in traction and wife at his bedside, four hundred miles from home and the children—fully understood the responsibilities entailed in forgiving. They may not have had the theological vocabulary to talk about forgiveness, but their lives embodied any truth that forgiveness is.

When they had the chance to scissor this man out of their lives, they chose to become involved; when they could have retaliated, they chose, instead, to care; when they might have been self-righteous, they leaned to understand and to set another person free to love.

Love is never wasted, and this special rarefied form of love—forgiving love—seals the world perpetually to its destiny. When forgiveness occurs, an event of cosmic proportions takes place: divisions are healed and the world moves closer to the state in which it was created.

TIME   She was a Christian from infancy, but at twenty-nine, Ruth Stapleton went on a retreat that changed her life.[5] During the course of that retreat, Mrs. Stapleton asked to be prayed for—a simple prayer that some relationships in her life be healed. After the service, she returned to her cabin disappointed that she felt no different as a result of the prayers for healing. That, as it turned out, was a premature assessment.

During the course of that night, Mrs. Stapleton was awakened by her mother who in turn had been awakened by her daughter's screams. "I had no notion that I was screaming," Mrs. Stapleton said, "but my mother said that there were bloodcurdling screams that she was afraid would awaken people in the other cabins scattered throughout the grounds." Groggily, she returned to sleep, only to be awakened twice again by her mother, her sister, and people from the other cabins, yards away, who heard her screams.

Mrs. Stapleton believes that retreat experience was the beginning of an experience of forgiveness that touched people and painful memories in her past. For days and months afterwards, she relived memories where she had spoken or judged harshly. She wrote, telephoned, and personally called on people, asking their forgiveness. Most of these healings took time before the relationships were whole again. For just one of them, a healing with a close relative, Mrs. Stapleton tells us that it took the better part of two years and that in many ways, it's still going on.

The rehabilitation process. It takes time. The healing process. The putting-together process. Because we don't see them as vividly as we see physical wounds, we may sense that inner spiritual wounds are healed before their time. Or we may want to rush a recovery, only to irritate the wound and extend the healing process in the long run.

We owe it to each other to recognize that the ability to forgive can't be rushed. We do a great disservice to our families and friends when we rush forgiveness because, in fact, simple time may be all that's needed to foster it.

One evening I received a call from a woman I know asking if I would be able to babysit for a five-year-old girl for the upcoming weekend. The woman was busying herself with finding a place for each of eight children to stay while the parents of these children, the telephone-caller's sister and husband, would go off on a "Marriage Encounter" weekend. The caller saw the weekend as the solution to the couple's recent marital distress.

As it turned out, we accepted the child for the weekend and the couple went off hurt, confused, resentful, and non-forgiving. The couple came back that way, too, to anxious friends and relatives who indicated their mighty disappointment that the weekend didn't "do the trick."

These people were rushed into a situation which was supposed to facilitate the forgiveness that everyone saw as necessary, without any regard, it seemed, for the fact that both these persons were hurting deeply, were hemorrhaging in a spiritual sense, and needed time to work out their feelings and let their hurts be healed.

It strikes me as the height of insensitivity to expect most people to be able to move quickly out of their new and intense pain and forgive those persons responsible for it. In my own experience I have found two types of people able to do this: people of uncommonly mature religious faith, like those we talk about in our last chapter; and persons who "appear" to be forgiving but who are so numbed by their pain that in fact they haven't yet scratched its surface. In this latter fold I have seen a woman who has continued to do her husband's laundry after he has indicated that he is filing for a divorce (even after he left the marital home), not because of a perduring, forgiving love for her spouse, but because the enormity of his confession hadn't permeated her consciousness and been made real.

The far more common behavior pattern is the one evidenced by the elder son in the parable of the prodigal son in Luke 15. After a typically rough day in the fields, the elder son hears music coming from the main house. When he inquires its purpose, he is told that a party honoring his younger brother is in full swing—the same younger brother who had absented himself from the farm and its responsibilities for a time long enough to make a difference to the older brother. Hurt and angered at the father who would allow such carousing, the elder brother cannot bring himself to participate in the festivities.

The elder brother in this parable may be refusing to forgive immediately, but he may also be asking for time. Not time as an excuse, but time as a way to come to terms with his hurts and with what has to be healed.

While I am led to believe that non-forgiving behavior is ultimately self-destructive, I am also convinced that being sufficiently in touch with our emotions when we have first been hurt, to recognize that hurt, is a much better place to start to deal with forgiveness than to deny the hurt outright without qualification.

Henri Nouwen has made a wise observation in this regard. We tend, he says, to value curing, solving people's problems, having people avoid pain to such a degree that sometimes curing supersedes caring.[6] Caring is the quality that lets me enter the pain of the other. That kind of caring provides a very supportive frame of reference for all of us. Probably the least helpful thing for me to have to face is disappointing my friends and family because I haven't gotten better fast enough.

Time. Simple time, Suffice it to say that it is critical in the forgiveness process.

WITNESSING OF THOSE WHO HAVE TRIED FORGIVENESS Imagine that someone came up to you today and told you this story:

"Ten years ago, when I was thirty and the mother of

four young sons, my husband deserted us. I had no job and no skills, so after a day of taking care of the children, I worked the night shift at a bakery across the street from our apartment building. I did that for ten years, and for every day during those ten years, I never forgot what my husband did to us. I hoped in my heart that he would be repaid some day by forces greater than mine; that he would be punished; that he would be unhappy; that he would suffer painfully for what he'd done."

What would you say?

Would you empathize with her bitterness, tell her you understood, that, really, there was nothing else she could do, that everyone understood, that her husband's behavior was reprehensible and stood outside the pale of forgiveness?

Or could you tell her a story from your life that might encourage her to forgive—not *because* you forgave—but because *when* you forgave, you became a lighter, happier, freer person?

If one of the reasons people don't forgive is that they don't have "heroes," or what we nowadays call "role models" in this forgiveness business, then the opposite must be true. If we had someone there ahead of us saying, "God knows, what you're living through is awful. It must be tearing you apart. But I can tell you from firsthand experience that my joy did not double when I tried retaliating; in fact, it shrank substantially. And I think I was one of the world's most miserable people. Before you commit yourself forever to non-forgiving, please consider an alternate approach. It worked for me. Maybe it'll work for you."

We can find our heroes in the most unlikely places. Some of the most compelling witnesses were made by readers in comments to Abigail van Buren ("Dear Abby") in an article in *McCall's* magazine some years ago.[7] Ms. van Buren recollects that she once published a letter asking, "If there is a reader somewhere who has caught her husband being unfaithful, has forgiven him, and has since had a happy marriage, would you please ask her to tell her story?"

To everyone's surprise, the letter received rapid and overwhelming responses. The gist of many of the letters was the same. One woman responded: "You will never know, unless you do both pray and forgive seventy times seven, what a grand and glorious thing it is to rise above the hurt." Others admitted that it wasn't easy to "forgive and forget," but they consistently recommended "the rewards of forgiveness, the futility of harboring a grudge."

More recently Christina Crawford has written a biography of her superstar mother, Joan Crawford.[8] The book puts to a lie the myth of the Hollywood magical kingdom provided to the four adopted children of this glamorous actress. Christina chronicles barbaric, frightening behavior of her mother, who went on tirades, abusing her children, threatening them, beating them, humiliating them.

Despite her own troubles, Christina believes that her younger brother Chris suffered even more. Until the age of twelve he was tied to his bed each night with a canvas harness, much like a straitjacket—pinned in the back—so that he would not be able to get out of bed during the night. ("It was a rule in our house that the children wouldn't get out of bed once they were put there," explains Christina.[9])

What interests me most about Christina Crawford's revelations is why she tells us she made them public: to let other children who have lived through similar nightmares know that they can survive, that they can make peace, and that they can forgive.

Christina confesses that she has forgiven her mother and that she "came to peace with what happened." After three years of therapy with Bernard Berkowitz and Mildred Newman, authors of *How to Be Your Own Best Friend*, many wounds had been healed. She hopes that her book will throw some light on the neglected area of child abuse.

"This was a story that needed to be told," she says. "There are hundreds or thousands of people who have lived through similar experiences. If I survived, others can too. They can change their lives."[10]

I don't know Christina Crawford, so I take her story at face value. But I do know men and women who were abused as children: children whose hands were burned and whose hair was pulled out by cruel, demented, or sick parents. And I know ungrateful and spoiled children who inflict gratuitous pain on well-meaning, decent parents. I know of many pained and painful relationships—and in the middle of the most impossible situations, I have seen the miracle of forgiveness take place.

Witnessing to this miracle is the most important legacy that Christina Crawford leaves with us.

CHAPTER VI

Forgivers

ROM THE BEGINNING they were an unusual group of people. They were born in Britain, but when they came to their mission in divided Rhodesia, they honored it as home. They shared surroundings, the water, the land with the natives; they gave themselves and all they had in return. They went about their work with enthusiasm and goodwill, yet they were not naive. They knew the risks: that their lives were in danger; that the political climate was severe; and that their Christian faith was on the line.

Rhodesians inured to the shallowness and selfishness of imported religions sensed something different among these decent and simple British missionaries. They sensed an honesty and a transparency: what they preached was what they lived.

What they preached was also how they died.

During the last days of June, 1978, eight of these missionaries and four of their children were battered to death by nationalist guerrillas.[1] They were buried after a funeral service that evoked powerful themes of forgiveness and redemption.

The leader of the mission and the subsequent religious speakers, representing some half dozen denominations and addressing over six thousand mourners at the funeral, stressed the work of the missionaries, their death as martyrs, and prayed that "those who have perpetrated such an action of shame might know grief and repentance and God's mercy." There were no references to the brutality of the murders, no calls for recriminations, nor any real mention of the guerrilla war or the disintegrating political situation in the country. The ministers and the mourners, demonstrating the fervor of their faith, and in a "spirit of forgiveness that contrasted sharply" with feelings elsewhere in the country, prayed simply that these people's deaths should not be in vain, and that a reconciliation could begin through the deaths of these people who always desired to be, and considered themselves to be, peacemakers.

This extraordinary display of forgiveness is ours to imitate. It would have qualified as forgiveness had it been less dramatic, less single-eyed in its fidelity to imitating the forgiveness of Christ, less joyful, and less immediate. It would still have been a forgiving act had the community of missionaries taken time to sort out their anger and loss. Apparently, the faith and love of this group of people was strong enough to offer a total gesture of reconciliation.

Jesus as Forgiver

Jesus not only preached, but practiced forgiveness. In one of his last conscious recorded activities, Jesus wrestled with the excruciating experience of forgiving his executioners: "Father, forgive them; they do not know what they are doing" (Luke 23:34). Far from being an isolated reference, the Gospel of Jesus frequently returned to this theme of forgiveness and taught in words and behavior that this response was going to be the bench mark of the follower of Christ.

For Jesus, forgiveness was a restorative event. In particular, forgiveness restored a relationship that had been displaced, broken, or destroyed through an ego-centered preoccupation that was sin. When forgiveness took place, it bonded and restored a person with God, and that bonding had a ripple effect that strengthened relationships with family and neighbors.

Jesus spent a fair amount of time heightening people's awareness of the existence of sin in their own lives that disabled relationships with others. His aim was less to impart new knowledge or more extensive learning about guilt, and more to induce each person to experience culpability, and in that experience to understand and revise a basic approach to their lives.

Then, as now, sin was an unpleasant and disturbing topic of conversation. Conversion, likewise, was a strenuous matter, and would-be converts offered the typical array of defense mechansims to delay, if not to stave off entirely, the change of heart that this prophet from Galilee called for.

The most frequent strategy that Jesus used to raise the level of consciousness about sin, disordered relationships, and the need for forgiveness, was the telling of parables.

Parables weren't invented by Jesus; they were popularly used toward the same end of conversion in the Old Testament as well. There, as in the New Testament, the purpose was to concretize in mundane, recognizable daily events an invisible or supernatural reality.

One of the chief advantages of parables was that they did not require making a frontal attack, thereby alienating an audience. Instead, the use of parables enabled the narrator to involve the listener in a predicament or situation that challenged the hearer to answer a question or solve a dilemma objectively and without prejudice. At the same time, the parable seductively called the listener's actions or lifestyle into question.

The effectiveness of a parable rested, principally, on the intelligibility of the story. The object, initially, was to offer an apparently objective case and to establish a common approach on which everyone agreed. Once a story had been skillfully selected and the hearer had been involved, the narrator could let the situation speak for itself.[2]

The dynamics of how a parable works are much akin to how a mirror functions in the life of an infant. Several years ago I was present when my eighteen-month-old daughter crawled to the living room sofa, climbed the cushions, and pulled herself up to the mirror hanging on the wall. Once there, she squealed and poked at the image, presuming she had found a playmate—just her size and of obviously similar temperament. As quickly as she could, she hurried down from the sofa to the wall behind the mirror where she expected to find her friend. What a puzzlement for a little baby to find no one there!

One afternoon, several days later, having reached the mirror, she placed the five fingers of her hand against it only to notice when she moved the hand away, the reflection moved away, too. In that process, she learned that this was *her* hand, *her* smile, *her* nose, eyes, and ears that she saw, and not a stranger, not someone else!

Parables function in a similar way. We are attracted, initially, to something or someone that we think is alien to us or to our lives. In our involvement, we poke around with the story, and we make judgments. The fact of the matter is that we judge our own cause without knowing that it is our own cause, until one day it occurs to us, as it occurs to the infant looking in the mirror, that we have, in this unexpected place, discovered ourselves. In this way, the parables allow Jesus to hold a mirror to people's lives. In that process, a disorder is recognized and the need for forgiveness is also seen.

Accounts Where Jesus Deals Directly with Sinners

Once that preparation is effected, Jesus can deal with individuals and their need for forgiveness. In the Gospels there are only six places where Jesus deals directly with sinners, a very small number of instances when we compare it with, for example, the healing narratives.[3] All but one of these stories appear in the Gospel of Luke; two other of the narratives have parallels in other Gospels as well.

The accounts where Jesus deals directly with sinners are the following.

THE HEALING OF THE PARALYTIC   (Mark 2:1–12 and parallels)

The victim was immobilized. He was a pathetic man carried about on a stretcher, yet, paradoxically, rich enough in friendships to have had near him those who sought his health—aggressively, at that—and who were faith-filled when they approached Jesus.

Astoundingly, Jesus first declared the man's sins forgiven, perhaps reaffirming the connection between physical and spiritual healing; perhaps owning that the spiritual paralysis was symptomatic of the physical disability. In any case, the significance of the action did not elude the audience: "Who can forgive sins but God alone?" (Mark 2:7) We can imagine the consternation of the witnesses: there is no doubt about what he's doing, yet only God should be doing it.

The history of Christianity documents long searches into Jesus' claims to divinity. Yet one of the clearest indications of a self-awareness of His divinity is Jesus' claim to effect the forgiveness of sins—a claim made with authority and decisiveness. At its core, what it implied was that the kingdom had already begun and was not only an eschatological promise.[4] The new age was here and its initiates were those who had submitted to fasting and penance before their baptism, effected for the remission of sins. And those invited to share the gift of forgiveness were those enlightened enough to understand their sinfulness by yielding their self-sufficiency and turning their "selves" to Him.

Some, like the paralytic, were obviously in need. Others would need the assistance and faith of their friends and communities before they made their declaration of dependence.

THE CALL OF SIMON PETER   (Luke 5:1–11)

Taking the Gospel words at their face value, one of the briefest and profoundest confessions in the New Testament was made by Peter. "Depart from me Lord, for I am a sinful man," is the confession of someone who had the courage to face his disordered being for what it was, because he was in the company of Jesus who would not hold him in contempt. Peter did not enumerate his sins by number and species, but his acknowledgment was no less trenchant or forgettable. In that loving, nonthreatening presence, Peter discovered God's goodness, his own sinfulness, and the possibility that he might become what he loved.

THE SINNER IN THE HOUSE OF SIMON   (Luke 7:35–50)

The setting of this story is unambiguous: A woman known to be of disreputable character appears at a dinner party hosted by Simon. She approaches Jesus and performs the humbling gesture of washing and anointing His feet. In the process, her emotional breakdown causes ample embarrassment to her host. The embarrassment is compounded by Simon's consternation. "How is it," he wonders, "that Jesus does not separate Himself from this woman. Why does He allow her ministrations when He knows—He *must* know—who she is."

This is a classic story of binding a person to his or her sin; of not being able to separate sin and sinner—for all, apparently, except Jesus. By allowing her to minister to Him and by acknowledging that ministry, Jesus shows that He (and His followers) need not fear the contamination of the sinner; that on the other hand, they have something to *offer* the woman. What Jesus offers is to unshackle and unburden the woman from a reputation that no one seemed willing to forgive and to forget. Jesus does that, and restores her self-worth and self-esteem in the bargain.

THE STORY OF ZACCHEUS   (Luke 19:1–10)

The Gospel introduces him as a sinner: "He (Jesus) has gone in to be the guest of a man who is a sinner" (ver. 7). While the sin isn't identified, we might guess that it may be connected with wealth that was illegally gained since Zaccheus promises, "Half of my goods I give to the poor, and if I have defrauded any one of anything, I restore it fourfold" (ver. 8).

Contact with Jesus enabled Zaccheus—as it enabled others—to change his ways. His purpose of amendment is more than words: Zaccheus is obviously willing to have it directly affect his life and lifestyle. Jesus, apparently, is satisfied with the offer of restitution and declares that salvation has come to Zaccheus's house. Apparently, too, the explicit mission of Jesus "to save the lost" (ver. 10) was accomplished and the occasion was for rejoicing.

THE CONVERSATION WITH THE THIEF ON THE CROSS (Luke 23:39–43)

Jesus ends His life where He spent most of it: in the midst of sinners. There are two thieves to be executed with Jesus, and Luke records that one of them acknowledged the discrepancy between the appropriateness of their punishment and the unmerited punishment of Jesus. "For we are receiving the due reward of our deeds, but this man has done nothing wrong" (ver. 41). It is that same thief who then asks, "Jesus, remember me when you come into your kingdom," (ver. 42) and Jesus is obviously receptive to the request. "Truly, I say to you, today you will be with me in paradise" (ver. 43).

The first major miracle of Jesus assures forgiveness to the paralytic. The last miracle before the death of Jesus assures a thief forgiveness and paradise.

THE WOMAN CAUGHT IN ADULTERY (John 8:1–11)

This is one of the several instances in the New Testament where Jesus is presented with a case to test His fidelity to Judaic law. An execution is at hand. A woman has been caught in the act of adultery and a group of people ask Jesus how He will deal with the issue. If He elects to free her, He disobeys the law; if He condemns her, His reputation as a compassionate teacher is tarnished, and possibly He stands at fault as one usurping a power that belongs to Rome.

In any event, Jesus doesn't appear confounded by the manipulative tactics of the bystanders. Once again, He sums up the problem in one word: sin. The sin He initially focuses on, however, is not the woman's sin, but everyone else's. Thus, He throws into question not the accused but the accusers, and He dismays them with His offer, "Let the one who is without sin among you be the first to throw a stone at her" (ver. 7).

Thus, Jesus binds the accusers to their sins to render them capable of repentance. On the other hand, He offers to free the accused woman from the weight of her shame and guilt by forgiving her sin.

The thread of these episodes forms a pattern and helps us look at why Jesus forgives and what the consequences of that forgiveness are. The fact of the matter is that Jesus made some rather sweeping claims about forgiveness. He established that forgiveness is an event, not only words, and He showed, through the way He offered forgiveness, the capacity to effect a significant change in the lives of the people He ministered to.

Why Jesus Forgives

Jesus forgives, very simply, because He is a free man; so radically and totally free, in fact, that He does not have to be concerned with losing face, with being hurt again, and He does not have to insist on a probation policy towards offenders. When Jesus forgives, it is an unconditional display of love and acceptance offered with no strings attached.

That kind of forgiveness brings on its heels a chain of explosive consequences.

What Happens When Jesus Forgives

When Hannah Arendt made the claim that "the discoverer of the role of forgiveness in the realm of human affairs was Jesus of Nazareth,"[5] she had in mind, most likely, the capacity of this kind of radical behavior to alter lives and situations.

There are, basically, five ways to explain what happens when Jesus forgives.

JESUS INITIATES THE ACT   Because Jesus is the first to see the possibilities of forgiveness in the realm of human affairs, we expect, and in fact, do find, that it is Jesus who initiates the act of forgiveness:

- The woman caught in the act of adultery has already been condemned. Her accusers present the woman to Jesus not as a penitent, not as one to be ministered unto, but rather as a case to test His knowledge of and fidelity to the Law. The woman herself makes no plea for forgiveness, yet Jesus offers nothing else.
- The woman at Simon's house *does* penance. She opens her heart to the Lord through gestures that indicate her gratitude for His presence, but she does not ask for forgiveness. Jesus invites her to that gift.
- The paralytic is brought to Jesus for a physical cure and he leaves with a spiritual one as well: "Thy sins are forgiven" (Mark 2:5).

We can dispose ourselves for merciful forgiveness like the woman at dinner at Simon's house; we can have our sins exposed like the adulterous woman; or we can use the metaphor of illness to confess our helplessness, disfigurement, or powerlessness, and then turn to Jesus. The point is that no one—not then, not now—is "deserving" of forgiveness. Maybe that's why no one ever thought of asking for it.

HE CONFERS SELF-ESTEEM AND SELF-WORTH   In that free initiative we see that Jesus goes a long way in restoring the self-respect and self-worth of those He forgives. The conferral of pardon, absolution, and forgiveness does precisely that: it claims that at the moment of advantage, we disavow the advantage that we have over someone and count that other as a brother or sister.

How does Jesus restore self-esteem? In several ways:

· To the woman caught in adultery, He chose not to judge her as others had, and moved her away from her sin and a death sentence.
· For the woman at the home of Simon, Jesus held up her behavior as exemplary. "You gave me no kiss, but from the time I came in she has not ceased to kiss my feet" (Luke 7:45).
· Jesus invited Himself to dine at Zaccheus's house and restored Zaccheus to his place as a "son of Abraham" (Luke 19:9).
· For the thief on the Cross, Jesus gifted paradise.
· Jesus' answer to Peter's avowal of sinfulness was to appoint him to a more important job. "Thou art Peter and upon this rock I will build my Church" (Matt. 16:18).

In all cases, Jesus' way was not to deal with people according to their sins as though their sins were going to say the last word about them. Instead, He chose to raise the repentant sinner to the special place at His right hand.

JESUS DEALS DECISIVELY WITH SIN   Another way of describing the paradigmatic forgiveness of Jesus is to say that it is a proclamation, a declaration of new life. Once again, this is a way of talking about forgiveness as an event marked by power.

The words most commonly used in the Old Testament for forgiveness are power words. Sin is

covered, put behind God's back so that it no longer stands in the way of a free exchange of love. Or it is carried away, so that the road is open.[6]

One of the more effective power words of the Old Testament invites us to consider that Yahweh will "remember our sins no more" (Ps. 103), that He will forget.

We get a sense of this activity of forgetting in the New Testament references where Jesus deals directly with sinners like Peter, Zaccheus, the woman at Simon's house, the woman caught in adultery, and the thief. We can sense in His proclamation to these people—and it is implied in His proclamation within some parables,[7] for example—that the past is just that—over and done with—and that it will not stand in the way of how Jesus relates to us. This is a difficult thing to trust, and takes practice at the beginning. Eventually, however, we come to live by this truth, and are able to incorporate it in our dealings with others. This, then, frees us from vengeance, which has the power to enclose "both doer and sufferer in the relentless automatism of the action process, which by itself need never come to an end."[8]

HE CANCELS A DEBT   True forgiveness always means that a debt has been canceled and that the slate has been wiped clean. When Hester Prynne is required to wear a scarlet letter *A* to acknowledge her adulterous behavior to the community,[9] we can safely assume that forgiveness has not been conferred and that her community perceived that a debt still remained to be paid.

To refuse to release the offender from the offense is an operational principle that contradicts what forgiveness is, since the Greek verb *aphienai*, which we translate as "to forgive," is actually to be translated as "to dismiss" or "to release."[10]

Jesus cancels a debt when He forgives, and He does more. Christians believe that the death of Jesus on the Cross is an act of atonement that, in fact, pays the debt for all sin from that event forward.

We can and should implore people to repent of individual or corporate injustices against Jews, blacks, American Indians, and numerous disadvantaged groups, and we can expect changes of lifestyle among the oppressors once repentance is under way. There is, however, no way that we can expect anyone to pay the full debt to the Jews for the massacre of six million of their own, or to any of the other people who have suffered staggering and brutal injustices, because there is simply no way that this kind of indebtedness can be satisfied. Yet Christians believe that the sufferings and death of the Son of God alone pay these debts, when these mysteries are coupled with a contrite heart and repentant spirit and the evil is denounced.

Christians believe that the Cross is a sign of something else, too. It stands as a sign of what it looks like when we refuse to love and to forgive. In those moments we are capable of destroying love itself, and we are capable of destroying all that is good in ourselves as well.

Through the Cross God shows us—God goes to great lengths to show us—our capacity for self-destruction. He chooses His son as if no other sign would do to illustrate the depth of His love and the importance of the message He wants to share: to refuse to forgive is to choose death of all that God loves and of all that is our happiness.

JESUS SHIFTS THE EMPHASIS FROM US TO GOD Lastly, to be forgiven rests as a transforming experience because it moves the center of attention from the self to someone else who chooses, in the face of our history of infidelity, to affirm, to treasure, and to care for us. That level of forgiveness transfigures.

Jesus never intended to focus the act of forgiveness on the sinner or to dwell on the wickedness that inspired the sin. Rather, the gospel nearly explodes with the startling mystery that God forgives. Jesus neither announces the depravity of the person nor a preoccupation with the past, but rather a prodigal love for his creatures and a looking forward to a future of forgiveness. It is a message that only the needy can hear; we can turn to it and understand something of its beauty and profundity after confessing helplessness. In the moment of need and destitution, He promises that the greatest of all gifts, forgiving love, is ours.

Shortly after the death of Jesus, Stephen followed in His Master's footsteps and asked forgiveness of his executioners: "Do not hold this sin against them" (Acts 7:60).

Through the intervening centuries we have accepted the testimony of other men and women bent on breaking the treacherous cycle of evil acts by freeing and forgiving their enemies. In the end, all forgivers do as Jesus did: they restore self-worth to the offender; they cancel a debt; they confer freedom; and they love beyond their imagining. The actual difficulty involved in putting the teachings of Jesus (on the subject of forgiveness) into practice, lies halfway between how simple it looks in the New Testament and how impossible it appears when we've been deeply hurt by someone. In time, those who forgive experience a freedom and peace that is so compelling and true to what it means to be alive and human, that the urge to retaliate lessens, and forgiveness becomes not an occasional deed but a lifestyle.

NOTES

INTRODUCTION

1. Hannah Arendt, *The Human Condition* (Chicago and London: University of Chicago Press, 1958), p. 237.
2. H.R. Mackintosh, *The Christian Experience of Forgiveness* (London: Nisbet and Co., Ltd., 1934), pp. 1–22.

I Bypassing Forgiveness

1. Corrie ten Boom, *The Hiding Place* (Old Tappan, N.J.: Fleming H. Revell Spire Books, 1971), p. 238.
2. See the Gospel of Luke, 15:11–32.

II Why People Don't Forgive

1. James N. Lapsley, "Reconciliation, Forgiveness, and Lost Contracts," *Theology Today* 23 (April 1966) pp. 44–59.
2. Louis Evely, *That Man Is You*, trans. Edmond Bonin (Westminster, Maryland: The Newman Press, 1965), pp. 92–93.
3. Martin Luther King, Jr., *The Strength to Love* (New York: Pocket Books, 1964), p. 33.
4. See the editorial, "Time to Die, Time to Love," in *The Tablet*, published as a diocesan newspaper in the Roman Catholic Diocese of Brooklyn, N.Y., July 13, 1978, p. 13.
5. Susan Sheehan, *A Prison and a Prisoner* (Boston: Houghton Mifflin, 1978).
6. Alex Haley, *Roots* (New York: Doubleday & Co., 1974), Chapter 84.
7. *Jeremiah* 18:2–6.
8. Douglas V. Steere (ed.), *Spiritual Counsels and Letters of Baron von Hügel* (London: Darton, Longman and Todd, 1959), p. 22.
9. See John Cassian, *De coenobiorum institutis* I (ca. 429) and *Conlationes* 2; *C.S.E.L.*, XVII, 81; 206ff and XIII, 121.
10. Alan Webster, *Broken Bones May Joy: Studies in Reconciliation and Resurrection* (London: SCM Press Ltd., 1968), p. 7.

NOTES

III   What Happens When People Don't Forgive

1. C.S. Lewis, *The Four Loves* (New York: Harcourt, Brace, 1960).
2. See John Powell, S. J., *Families* (Niles, Ill.: Argus Communications, 1978) for an excellent reflection on memories.
3. The most informative books on the subject of the healing of memories are: Morton Kelsey, *Healing and Christianity* (New York: Harper & Row, 1973) Dennis and Matthew Linn, *Healing Life's Hurts* (New York: Paulist Press, 1978); idem, *Healing of Memories: Prayer and Confession—Steps to Inner Healing* (New York: Paulist Press, 1974); Francis MacNutt, *Healing* (Notre Dame, Ind.: Ave Maria Press, 1974); idem, *Power to Heal* (Notre Dame, Ind.: Ave Maria Press, 1977); Agnes Sanford, *The Healing Light* (Plainfield, N.J.: Logos, 1947); Barbara Shlemon, *Healing Prayer* (Notre Dame, Ind.: Ave Maria Press, 1976). On the subject of healing through use of the active imagination, see Ruth Stapleton, *The Gift of Inner Healing* (Waco, Texas: Word, 1976); idem, *The Experience of Inner Healing* (Waco, Texas: Word, 1977).
4. Viktor Frankl, *Man's Search for Meaning* (New York: Washington Square Press, 1963).
5. Corrie ten Boom, *op. cit.*

6. See, for example, Mary Bosanquet, *The Life and Death of Dietrich Bonhoeffer* (London: Hodder and Stoughton, 1968), p. 278.
7. The Epistles to the Colossians, Philippians, Philemon, and Ephesians are traditionally regarded as having been written by Paul from prison. See, especially, Philippians 1:12–26 and Colossians 1:24–2:4.
8. Henri Nouwen, *With Open Hands* (Notre Dame, Ind.: Ave Maria Press, 1975), p. 12.
9. Alfred Adler, *A Study of Organ Inferiority and Its Psychical Compensation: A Contribution to Clinical Medicine?* (New York: N.Y. Nervous and Mental Disease Publishing Co., 1917).
10. Meyer Friedman and Ray Rosenmann, *Type A Behavior and Your Heart* (Greenwich, Conn.: Fawcett, 1974).
11. O. Carl Simonton and Stephanie S. Simonton, "Belief Systems and Management of Malignancy," *Journal of Transpersonal Psychology* VII, No. 1 (1975), pp. 29–47.
12. Gabriel Marcel, *Creative Fidelity*, trans. Robert Rosthal (New York: Farrar, Straus, 1964).
13. C.G. Montefiore and H. Loewe (eds.), *A Rabbinic Anthology* (New York: Meridian Books, 1938), pp. 317–318.
14. In this regard, see Psalms 3, 6, 7, 9, 10, 17, 18, 22, 26, 31, 34, 38, 55, 59, 77, 90, 109.
15. Paul Tillich, *The Courage to Be* (New Haven and London: Yale University Press, 1968), p. 166.

IV   Forgiveness

1. C. G. Montefiore and H. Loewe (eds.), *op cit.*, pp. 462-463.
2. W. Telfer, *The Forgiveness of Sins* (London: SMC Press Ltd., 1959), p. 9.

NOTES

See also Alan Webster, *Broken Bones May Joy* (London: SCM Press Ltd., 1968), p. 14.

3. Glen Gersmehl, "The Vision of Cesar Chavez," *Christianity and Crisis* 30 (January 11, 1971)pp. 296–300.

4. Hannah Arendt, *op. cit.*, p. 241.

5. Andras Angyal, "The Convergence of Psychotherapy and Religion," *Journal of Pastoral Care* V (1952)p. 13.

6. *Ibid:* "This fulcrum may be at the beginning as small as a mustard seed, but it can develop and branch out, becoming a strong and vital organization. There may come a time when the patient will value this fulcrum or foothold in health, as a 'pearl of great price' for which he is willing to exchange his neurotic way of life, with all its fears and all its deceptive temptations."

7. John Powell, *Why Am I Afraid to Tell You Who I Am?* (Niles, Ill.: Argus Communications, 1969).

8. C. G. Jung, *The Archetypes and the Collective Unconscious*, vol. IX of the *Collected Works* (Princeton: Princeton University Press, 1959–1968), p. 20.

9. *Ibid.*

10. Bernard Bro, *On demande des péchés* (Paris: Editions du Cerf, 1972).

11. Hannah Arendt, *op. cit.*, p. 241.

12. *Ibid.*, pp. 242-243.

13. H.R. Mackintosh, *op. cit.*

14. Rollo May, *Love and Will* (New York: W.W. Norton & Company, Inc., 1969), p. 172.

15. Rollo May, *op. cit.*, p. 173.

16. John Claypool, "The Event of Forgiveness," Broadway Baptist Church Sermons, Forth Worth, Texas, XII, No. 23 (October 14, 1973) p. 4

17. Charles B. Hanna, *Face of the Deep* (Philadelphia: Westminster Press, 1967), p. 95.

18. Dietrich Bonhoeffer, *Life Together*, trans. John W. Doberstein (New York: Harper & Row, 1954), p. 116.

19. *The Rite of Penance* (Washington, D.C.: Publications Office, United States Catholic Conference, 1975).

20. James T. Burtchaell, *Philemon's Problem* (Chicago: Life in Christ, 1973), p. 154.

21. Elizabeth O'Connor, *Search for Silence* (Waco, Texas: Word, 1977), p. 29.

22. Henri Nouwen, "Generation without Fathers," *Commonweal* (June 12, 1970) p. 50.

23. Dennis Linn and Matthew Linn, *Healing Life's Hurts* (New York: Paulist Press, 1978), pp. 123–124.

24. *Ibid.*

25. David E. Roberts, *Psychotherapy and a Christian View of Man* (New York: Charles Scribner's Sons, 1950), p. 135.

26. *Ibid.*

V What Enables Forgiveness

1. Andras Angyal, *op. cit.*, p. 10.

2. Hannah Arendt, *op. cit.*, p. 240.

3. Two helpful references are John Powell, *Why Am I Afraid to Love?* (Niles,

Ill.: Argus Communications, 1967) and Willard Gaylin, *Feelings: Our Vital Signs* (New York: Harper & Row, 1978).

4. Seward Hiltner, "The Defining of Pastoral Theology," *Religion in Life* XXVIII (1959) p. 499.

5. Ruth Carter Stapleton, *Inner Healing*, a cassette tape recording, Tape I, Side 2, (Waco, Texas: Word, 1976).

6. Henri Nouwen, *Out of Solitude* (Notre Dame, Ind.: Ave Maria Press, 1974), especially pp. 31–57.

7. See *McCall's* (January, 1963), p. 103.

8. Christina Crawford, *Mommie Dearest* (New York: William Morrow, 1978).

9. *Ibid.*, p. 53.

10. See the article-interview of Eleanor Hoover with Christina Crawford in *People* 10, No. 23 (December 4, 1978)p. 47.

VI Forgivers

1. This account is based on the news story "Missionaries in Rhodesia Bury Dead Without Rancor," by Michael T. Kaufman reported in *The New York Times*, Friday, June 30, 1978, p. A2.

2. See the excellent study by Arnold Uleyn, "Parables: an indirect method of bringing man to confess his sin," in *Is It I, Lord?* (New York: Holt, Rinehart and Winston, 1969) Chapter 3, for which I am indebted in this brief treatment of parables.

3. William Klassen, *The Forgiving Community* (Philadelphia: Westminster Press, 1966), pp. 112–134 holds that there are seven occasions where Jesus deals directly with sinners. Klassen includes the denial of Peter recorded in Luke 22:31 ff., 61.

4. See the interesting study by Hans Freiherr von Campenhausen, *Kirchliches Amt und Geistliche Vollmacht* (Tübingen, 1953), especially pp. 8–11. Cf. also Paul Tillich, *The Courage to Be, op. cit.*, pp. 164–167 indicating Jesus' concern with the here and now.

5. Hannah Arendt, *op. cit.*, p. 238.

6. Alan Webster, *op. cit.*, p. 10.

7. For a closer study of this subject, see Joachim Jeremias, *The Parables of Jesus*, trans. S. H. Hook (New York: Charles Scribner's Sons, 1962), pp. 124–146.

8. Hannah Arendt, *op. cit.*, p. 241.

9. Nathaniel Hawthorne, *The Scarlet Letter* (New York: Random House Modern Library edition, 1926).

10. See, in this regard, Heinrich Ebeling, *Griechisch-deutsches Wörterbuch zum Neuen Testamente* (1923). On this subject, see also Klassen, *op. cit.*, pp. 111–112.

INDEX